D1560146

WALKER PERCY *remembered*

DAVID HORACE HARWELL

# Walker Percy

## *remembered*

A Portrait

in the Words

of Those Who

Knew Him

The University of

North Carolina Press

Chapel Hill

This book was published with the assistance of the
Fred W. Morrison Fund for Southern Studies of the
University of North Carolina Press.

The paper in this book meets the guidelines for
permanence and durability of the Committee on
Production Guidelines for Book Longevity of the
Council on Library Resources.

Library of Congress Cataloging-in-Publication Data
Walker Percy remembered : a portrait in the words of
those who knew him / David Horace Harwell.
    p. cm.
Interviews with Walker Percy's family, close friends,
and acquaintances, by David Horace Harwell.
Includes bibliographical references (p. ) and index.
ISBN-13: 978-0-8078-3039-0 (cloth : alk. paper)
ISBN-10: 0-8078-3039-9 (cloth : alk. paper)
1. Percy, Walker, 1916–  2. Novelists, American—20th
century—Biography.  3. Philosophers—United States—
Biography.  4. Physicians—United States—Biography.
I. Harwell, David Horace.
PS3566.E6912Z97 2006
813'.54—dc22    2006005169

10 09 08 07 06   5 4 3 2 1

*To*

Dr. William A. Sullivan

*(1942–2003),*

*my beloved teacher, mentor,*

*and friend*

# Contents

# Acknowledgments

I am pleased to have this opportunity to thank the many colleagues, friends, and faculty members who have helped me with this book. I am most indebted to Philip Beidler of the University of Alabama, who helped guide me through the birthing process of the text, for his patience and wisdom and most of all for giving me lots of latitude. Sian Hunter of the University of North Carolina Press has been the most wonderful editor an author could ask for and has made the publication process astonishingly smooth and pleasant. I also wish to thank Bertram Wyatt-Brown for sharing his knowledge and opinions with candor and for lending his support to the publication of the manuscript. Of special note as well are Salli Davis, Bill Ulmer, Metka Zupancic, and Michael Martone of the University of Alabama for their invaluable input, inspiring questions, and encouragement.

This book would not have been possible without the support of the faculty members at Winthrop University who raised me from academic infancy. I have said many times over, and I am happy to repeat in print, that Winthrop University is one of the finest schools a young academic can be trained at, both as a scholar and a teacher, and I am very grateful to my academic family there.

For sharing their thoughts and granting their permission to publish these conversations, I owe special thanks to the cast of characters found in this book who are among the many fascinating people with whom Walker Percy surrounded himself. I am particularly grateful to Percy's brothers, LeRoy and Phin Percy, who provide a close familial perspective on the author's life; to Shelby Foote, who by any measure should be considered a brother of Percy's as well; and to Bunt Percy, Percy's wife, who referred me to many family friends in the community. Bunt respectfully declined to be interviewed for this project, on behalf of herself and her two daughters, explaining that they prefer to save their memories of Walker for themselves. It is not surprising that she would desire privacy after the many interviews, awards ceremonies, and conferences she has endured, but I deeply regret that her stories are not among those collected here.

Finally, I wish to acknowledge the contribution of William A. Sullivan to this book. When Bill was a young boy living in Covington, Louisiana, he used to deliver newspapers along Jahncke Avenue. One of his throws was to a "Dr. Percy." Bill said of this fellow that "at the time, nobody knew who he was, only that he didn't work for a living." Bill grew up to be a professor of English, and by the time he arrived at Winthrop University, he knew exactly who Walker Percy was. He held a strong affection for all of his students, including me, and he saw in my life many similarities to his own. We were both raised in the families of southern ministers, we both struggled at a young age with whether to follow such an unusual legacy, and we both found ourselves trying to make sense of the world through the study of literature. Our common experience growing up in the South was why Bill first encouraged me to read Walker Percy's fiction. He was right—I loved it.

As my education progressed into doctoral studies, Bill shared with me his desire to write a monograph on Percy's idea of the "holiness of the ordinary," a question Percy had posed in various forms about just how a person can make it through a life filled with the oppression of ordinary Tuesday afternoons. By that time, I had read Percy's nonfiction and Jay Tolson's *Pilgrim in the Ruins*, and I shared with Bill my desire to perform biographical research in the southern tradition of storytelling by gathering some sort of oral history about Percy. Not long afterward, I learned that Bill was in the early stages of a disease related to Parkinson's. I drove him to visit the Percy archives in Chapel Hill, and we discussed making a foray to Covington to gather material for our projects. We made the trip—two trips, in fact. By this time, however, Bill's health had begun to fail, and he said to me late one evening, exhausted after a day of accompanying me to visit Percy's friends and neighbors, that he didn't know if he would ever complete his project but that he hoped I would continue my plans. Bill never did get to write his book, but our two trips together gave me two things that I value quite highly. I began to collect material for this book, and I got to ride through Mississippi and Louisiana with Bill and see the places where he had grown up, learn how much more we had in common, hear his stories, and cement practically a father-son relationship. Bill Sullivan had a great mind and a great heart. Many people were saddened to see him go into a steep decline and finally leave us on 11 April 2003. I have dedicated these pages to him, just as he dedicated his career to mentoring me and many others.

WALKER PERCY *remembered*

Looking for Walker Percy

Many people cried when they talked to me about Walker Percy. This was a bit surprising at first. When I set out to fill in some of the gaps in the Percy story, I was expecting stories and laughter, the primary elements I thought were missing from the biographies already written on Percy's life. Invariably, however, the conversations turned to thoughts of Percy's absence from the lives of the people who shared their stories with me, remembrances of his passing, and there was sadness in those memories. He was a much-loved man, and his loss is still felt by those who were close to him.

This project has been called a number of things: an oral history, a biographical collage, a community biography. What it is, in essence, is a glimpse at how Percy lived his life, taken from a number of different perspectives. The intended result is that this collection of stories told by people who were close to Percy, stories that often complement and sometimes contradict each other but always illuminate, will create a rich portrait of the man. The participants in this community biography were allowed to speak at length about themselves, as well as their relationships to Percy. Their stories have been left unaltered to reveal what sort of people made up the structure of Percy's life.

As for the stories here, the one that is not presented is that of Percy's life in its entirety. Two biographies have been published on Percy: Jay Tolson's *Pilgrim in the Ruins* and Patrick Samway's *Walker Percy: A Life*. Shelby Foote agreed with my assessment of the two works when I called to ask him to speak with me about Percy. I told him simply that I thought some good stories might have been left out. Foote added:

> I don't think, and there's nothing unusual about this, I don't think anybody will ever really get Walker into a biography. Jay Tolson came closest, but even that didn't get it all. There's a funnier side to Walker that never gets into the book. He could be sardonic in all kind of ways, like one time when we were sitting on his porch, and this fella named Charley Something who walked funny, he was messed up and all bent over, came by. Walker looked across and he

said, "You know, ain't nothing wrong with Charley. He just doesn't give a damn." He was like that.

But there is much more than Percy's humor to explore. My work is a response to these two biographies, an attempt to flesh out the character of the author in the context of his community, his closest friends, and his family. The stories are presented with very little authorial interference beyond introductory material, though there is constant authorial guidance to the conversations. I wanted to find out more about some of the people with whom Percy surrounded himself and to allow these people to construct their own biographical profiles of the man.

## MILESTONES IN PERCY'S LIFE

Although readers of either Tolson's or Samway's book will already know the story of Percy's life, it seems prudent to include a summary here.

Walker Percy was born in the still-young city of Birmingham, Alabama, at St. Vincent's Hospital on 28 May 1916, the first child of Mattie Sue Phinizy Percy and LeRoy Pratt Percy. At the time of his birth, the nation was engaged in a heated debate over whether to join Britain in war, and Walker's father had just written an editorial for the *Birmingham Age-Herald* arguing against U.S. involvement.

Walker Percy was born into a household beset by troubles. On 8 February 1917, when Percy was less than nine months old, his grandfather, also named Walker Percy, succumbed to depression. Having returned home from Baltimore, interrupting his treatment for the disease, the elder Walker Percy shot himself in the chest with his twelve-gauge shotgun in the attic of his home. Though the *Age-Herald* reported the incident as a gun accident, it was accepted quietly by the family and the community that the elder Walker had committed suicide.

Seven years later, in 1925, LeRoy Pratt was suffering from serious bouts of depression and anxiety himself, a condition that Percy would later refer to as "the Crouching Beast." Percy borrowed this term from Henry James's short story, "The Beast in the Jungle" (1907), which, as Bertram Wyatt-Brown points out in *The House of Percy: Honor, Melancholy, and Imagination in a Southern Family*, was a story occasioned by the suicide in Venice of James's good friend Constance Woodson. Le-Roy Pratt had sought treatment at Johns Hopkins University's Phipps Psychiatric Clinic after he had attempted suicide by cutting his wrists. In 1929, LeRoy Pratt Percy shot himself in the chest with his father's shotgun in the attic of his own home, a mirror-image of his father's suicide. Walker, age thirteen, and LeRoy, age twelve, received word at a summer camp near Chicago and returned home. Phin, age eight, had been in the house with his mother when the gun went off.

After the funeral, the boys and their mother went briefly to her parents' home in Athens, Georgia, before being invited to live in Greenville, Mississippi, with their cousin Will Percy, a lawyer and planter and son of the late Senator LeRoy Percy. "Uncle Will," as he came to be called because of the age difference between him and the Percy boys, was to become the new dominant force in the boys' lives. A war hero, a notable figure during the 1927 Mississippi River flood, and an accomplished writer and poet, Uncle Will welcomed the boys to their new home, but it was not long before tragedy struck again. Mattie Sue became withdrawn following her husband's death. Descriptions suggest that she was suffering from depression herself by 1930, when she took her boys to Greenville. On the Saturday after Easter in 1932, she went for a drive with Phin, then age ten, to look for LeRoy, who had gone bicycle riding with a friend. Patrick Samway relates what happened:

As she drove onto the small wooden Black Bayou bridge, the car suddenly plunged into Deer Creek. It was twelve-thirty in the afternoon. Panic-stricken, Phin grabbed for his mother, who had reached out to hold him. His adrenalin pumped as he looked at his trapped mother; her foot seemed to have been lodged between the brake and the accelerator pedals. With very little air left in his lungs, he scrambled out through a window. Phin was delirious as he realized that his efforts to help his mother had been futile. . . . They tried for over an hour to revive Mattie Sue, but to no avail. When Will arrived, he had Phin driven back. LeRoy and his friend arrived at the scene on their bicycles after the ambulance had passed them and were absolutely stunned. LeRoy could not control his grief. Walker was riding in a car not far away when he learned of the accident. When he reached Deer Creek a guard recognized him and would not let him approach very close. (54–55)

Samway goes on to reveal that questions arose as to whether Mattie Sue had intentionally driven off the bridge in an act of suicide. Such an action was even more troubling in light of the fact that Phin, her youngest child, was in the car with her. Though others insist that her death was caused by either driver error or even a heart attack, Walker revealed years later that he had always thought his mother's death was suicide. An anonymous source told me and another biographer that Phin had the impression that his mother had tried to hold him in the car and that he actually had to fight his way out of the vehicle.

The three boys, at the tender ages of sixteen, fifteen, and ten, found themselves delivered into a world of depression, traumatic death, and uncertainty. It is no surprise that, at this early age, Walker befriended the young Shelby Foote of Greenville, who had also lost his father tragically. Their friendship would last for the rest of their lives. Walker Percy went on to the University of North Carolina at Chapel Hill, then to Columbia University Medical School, and finally to Bellevue Hospital in New York City, where he was an intern in pathology in 1942. There he encountered his next great tests: Uncle Will, the anchor of the family, died, and shortly afterward, Walker contracted tuberculosis from a cadaver. Percy, at the age of twenty-six, faced the loss of another parental figure, the end of his medical career, the decline of his health, and the beginning of a two-year stay in a sanatorium in Lake Saranac, New York. LeRoy and Phin were serving in World War II, LeRoy with the army and Phin with the navy. Walker, mostly flat on his back for twenty-four months, started to read. After years of studying scientific texts, Walker turned primarily to the works of existential philosophers and novelists, the beginning of a lifelong effort to make sense out of the strange and tragic world into which he had been thrown.

After a few years of recuperation and wondering what to do with his life, Percy married Mary Bernice "Bunt" Townsend on 7 November 1946. In the coming years, the Percys converted to Catholicism and began a family in Covington, Louisiana. Percy also established himself as a writer, winning the National Book Award for his first published novel, *The Moviegoer*, in 1961. It was the beginning of a remarkable career of letters in the humanities, both fiction and nonfiction, in which Percy's protagonists always seemed to mirror his own life, that of the eternal wanderer or wayfarer, the pilgrim on a quest for meaning. Before his passing in 2003, LeRoy Percy, Walker's younger brother, had the following exchange with me about this distinguishing characteristic of his brother, which is discussed at length in the conversation with LeRoy later in this book:

> Well, everything that Walker wrote about—not everything, but most everything—can be summed up in one word: the search. He was always looking for what the hell the story was.
> *Was that just Walker's way of thinking?*
> No, I think it affects everybody. Who the hell knows what the deal is? Do you?
> *Certainly don't.*
> Well, one thing you'll do is, you'll search and try to find out, right? Hell, I think that's what was the underlying theme of his books.
> *Do you think he ever reached a peaceful resolution for his search?*
> I don't know. It may be that the church taught him, I just don't know. I can't answer that.
> *What about you?*
> Walker used to say, "Roy, you're a real dog. You're like the guy who sits in a rocking chair on the front porch of a church. You're scared to go in, but you don't want to be too far away, just in case."

Until his death from cancer in 1990, Walker Percy was regarded as a source of wisdom by intellectual seekers, religious wanderers, and the existentially confused. His writings combine a serious preoccupation with life and death, philosophical matters, and religion with dark humor and irony.

Walker Percy was a slightly built man and by many accounts quiet as well. His movement across the earth, however, is still felt very strongly. He is said to have been fascinated with conversation and to have scrutinized anyone who fell under his gaze for what they thought of the "big issues" of life. It is with similar motives that I went looking for Walker Percy, to find out more about what sort of man he was, to hear from those in his community who knew him, and to gather the stories by which he is remembered.

My search for Walker Percy began in 1995 when I was working for a national organization of college English teachers. My work involved planning events for a conference in New Orleans, and Bill Sullivan of Winthrop University, who had lived in Covington during part of his childhood and again as an adult, suggested that a few members of the board might want to make a trip to Covington, a sort of pilgrimage to see where Percy had lived his adult life as a writer. We were put into contact with Lee Binnings Barrios, who had served as an administrative assistant to Percy for several years. Barrios was very helpful, and she even contacted Percy's wife, Bunt, to see if a few scholars could come to Jahncke Avenue to see the house on the Bogue Falaya River where Percy had spent his years as an author. An itinerary was planned that included stops at the Percy home; the Kumquat, a bookstore owned by the Percys' daughter; the cemetery at St. Joseph Abbey, where Percy is buried; and Bechac's, the restaurant in Mandeville overlooking the north shore of Lake Pontchartrain where Percy and many friends met weekly for dinner.

The news of this small excursion caused quite a stir among those planning to attend the conference, and a few more people were invited. A special seminar on Percy was added to the closing day of the conference, and as one thing led to another, the small party of Percy devotees grew into a group of over 120 college English teachers. The group set out in two chartered buses for Covington on a Percy Pilgrimage on a Saturday afternoon in April. Bunt Percy, it turned out, was still expecting a carload.

Thankfully, Bunt is a kind woman. She stood by graciously as two buses and a few cars came up her driveway, and she even invited everyone to walk through the home, answering questions all the while. The house was thoroughly inspected, the bookstore dutifully plundered, and the restaurant nearly ransacked. The trip was a smashing success.

Covington and Mandeville are special places. On more than a few occasions after the Percy Pilgrimage, Bill Sullivan and I discussed whether Bunt would be willing to receive us again should we reappear to do some type of research. It turned out that she was willing, and she mentioned a few people we might talk to about Percy. Each in turn suggested another person, and the search was on.

A look at the table of contents of this book will suggest the various perspectives from which these stories of Percy are told. The variation in perspective makes for an interesting case of triangulation on the nature of the author. The text reveals Percy in relation to those he knew and thus provides a series of varying profiles of the author. For example, Percy has been labeled a "Catholic novelist." He was raised a Protestant and converted to Catholicism from a primarily agnostic point of view in his early adulthood, served on a number of church projects, and was even buried at St. Joseph Abbey in Covington, having been named an oblate of the church. Some of Percy's friends and family members believe that, in the words of Shelby Foote, "the church was really an answer for him." Foote continued: "What's more, he was interested in a very serious way. He truly studied the Bible, which his father had done before him, especially Revelations. He read Aquinas, and read all the modern philosophers, like Maritain, to their depths. I always thought that he made other Catholics feel like they were Baptists because he knew the church so well."

Others were not so convinced that Percy had found answers in the church. One person openly wept when talking about Percy's death and asked that I stop taping the conversation. She said she hoped he found some sort of answer because he had been searching for answers his entire life and she feared that he had to lie alone on his deathbed with no comfort from God or man. Another stopped the tape recorder and said that Bunt may have successfully converted to Catholicism but that Bunt had never really understood Percy and neither she nor the church was capable of giving him the type of intellectual comfort he needed. A former Catholic priest, James Boulware, said that Percy was

a wanderer, no question. A sovereign wayfarer. I want to say this gently: Walker was lost in the sense that he saw so much ambivalence. Not just "lost in the cosmos," but he—I guess this brings together a bunch of opinions I have about Walker that I don't mean in terms of criticism, just in terms of observation: I don't think Walker was ever comfortable as a Catholic. He was not really, completely Catholic. Walker was still Protestant, but he saw through the kind of thin veil that you find in Protestantism, and he saw the richness of the Catholic church, but he also saw through the pomp and circumstance that was there that didn't compute to any more exceptional meaning than did the overly individualistic Protestant ethic and its peculiar conflicts. I think he had these conflicts all along. He was searching.

Such differences of opinion enrich this book as they reveal the story of Percy's life. Also found in these stories are a number of anecdotes about Percy's writing process and his ways of relating to members of the community from various religious, ethnic, and socioeconomic backgrounds. Perhaps most important, Percy's friends and the citizens of Covington relate here for the first time a wealth of information about his involvement in civil rights work in Covington.

The conversations with "Red" Smith and Carrie Cyprian offer a glimpse of Percy from members of the Covington community, a community Percy described in his essay "Why I Live Where I Live" as a "non-place," a place of "average everydayness," the type of place Percy desperately needed to balance his constant preoccupation with the life of the mind. Carrie Cyprian, the Percys' housekeeper, provides a unique perspective on daily life in the Percy household. Further, she became a connection for Percy to the African American community in Covington. We learn in the course of conversations with her and others that Percy was very involved in helping African Americans in the community rise above the social and economic barriers they encountered at the time. Cyprian's remark that the Percys introduced her to other people as their "friend" instead of calling her their housekeeper or their maid is a priceless detail about Percy's commitment to civil rights. Also, the conversation took place at her lovely country home, which she financed through the credit union that Percy helped establish.

The interview with Red Smith approaches the subject of civil rights in Covington as well, though gingerly. Smith ended his talk on tape with me shortly after the subject came up, but after the tape recorder was turned off, he spoke for some time about the "Alabama troubles" and the Wallace era. I learned that Smith and his father owned the shotgun houses that African Americans rented in Covington for many decades because most were unable to get financing for homes before

Percy and others founded the credit union. Leroy Frick discussed with me life in those shotgun houses, the founding of the credit union, and how Smith mellowed over the years and worked to get roads paved in the area. One detail that I included in the Red Smith interview involved an exchange between Smith and a black man who came into his hardware store during the interview. This brief exchange is significant because it is a classic example of the type of interaction that developed between the races once back-door business for African Americans was abolished.

All of these conversations, these sometimes contradictory variations in perspective, call attention to the fact that biographical research and writing do not result in capturing the "truth" or the "essence" of an individual. Rather, the process of writing anything that is biographical in nature is not so much an act of discovering truths as an act of constructing myths. These myths, furthermore, may have some basis in empirical fact, but the telling and retelling of a story always involve the process of myth-making. Percy's biographers usually cast him in the mythical role of tragic hero, sage, or prophet, none of which precisely fit.

### INFLUENCES

One of the resources that spurred my study of the life of Walker Percy was *Talking about William Faulkner*, a series of recollections and anecdotes gathered by Faulkner's nephew, Jimmy Faulkner, during visits with two scholars to important sites used as settings in Faulkner's work. In preparing to research Percy, I knew from reading this text and from later meeting Jimmy Faulkner that I wanted to construct some type of oral history about Percy.

In his article "Biography: Inventing the Truth" in John Batchelor's *The Art of Literary Biography*, Richard Holmes says that biography is a "mongrel subject," a beast that is hard to tame and make behave as we want it to. It does not often follow genre rules, if there really are such rules, and the various forms of biography do not fall neatly into categories. Of more interest to me, however, is Holmes's analysis of why one writes about another person's life to begin with; be it hero worship or hero denunciation, Holmes suggests, chronicling a life requires a very personal motivation.

Justin Kaplan says, in reference to his biography *Mr. Clemens and*

*Mark Twain*, that he was drawn to Twain because the personal hardship Twain endured in his youth was akin to that of Kaplan's own youth. Kaplan admits that he found himself empathizing with Twain's desire to flee the physical and emotional trappings of a difficult childhood and thus begins the story of Twain at the age of thirty.

My desire to research the life of Walker Percy comes from similar empathies. What drew me to Percy first were his sense of dark humor and his relentless pursuit of existential questions in his novels. Then when I read Jay Tolson's *Pilgrim in the Ruins*, I was captivated by the story of a young man who endured two, possibly three, family suicides before he was sixteen years old, resulting in the loss of his grandfather and both of his parents and the attendant bouts of depression, anxiety, and existential angst that turned his life's journey into a search for meaning, for the existence of a deity, and for a stable manner of living. I had experienced similar problems during my own childhood and youth, including deaths of family members and bouts of mental illness in our household, and I grew to love Percy's work and his life story in the way that one loves a friend who seems to understand the worst parts of you because he's been there himself. What also drew me to Percy was his penchant for studying philosophy, particularly existential questions, while also being able to relate such questions to ordinary people. I had great admiration for a man who had lived through tragedies and had studied great works of literature and philosophy but still puttered around town in his little red pickup truck, eating Popeye's chicken or going to the Waffle House — a template for good living if ever there was one.

Paula Backscheider, in her book *Reflections on Biography*, insists that the biographer's authorial voice "need not be authoritative, or magisterial," or written in any way that suggests that it has captured the singular essence of an individual. In doing my work on Percy, I thought I would find some new narrative thread about him that I could relate to other readers. What I had not considered fully, until I had a conversation with the first of several of Percy's friends, was giving up the authorial voice almost completely. One of scholar and biographer Leon Edel's most well-known suggestions for engaging in biography is that the biographer must find a form that suits his or her subject; when I sat down with a glass of bourbon and a former priest who had a great deal to say about Percy, I found the form that

I think best suits Percy. The former priest said that Percy was an avid conversationalist and that he spent the majority of his time probing nearly every acquaintance, like the physician he was, for evidence of spiritual pathology or health, for ideas about important subjects. I decided to continue with the part of my research that involved conversations with those who had known Percy and to let those conversations speak for themselves. This muting of the authorial voice was to me the essence of what I might share with a reader because it allowed the reader to hear what I heard about the subject.

I do not resist the notion that literary biography, meaning both biography about literary figures and biography written in a literary form, should follow the arc of a given story, suppress certain facts and emphasize others. All biography is a construction of some sort, to be sure. What I found, though, was that, given a willing party—and all of mine were certainly that—the people who knew Percy tended to construct their own mythologies about Percy, about themselves, and about themselves in relation to Percy. The result was an oral history that could be called a community biography, a life defined by its human environment, which emerged as a series of conversations about a man who lived for just such conversations.

## James Boulware, Former Priest

MANDEVILLE, LOUISIANA

*James Boulware, a former priest at St. Joseph Abbey, lives just off the north shore of Lake Pontchartrain in Mandeville, Louisiana. His house is built in the traditional Acadian style, a style that remains popular in the region. The interior is very handsome and largely made of natural wood, as is the furniture. He explained that he built most of the house and its furniture himself. When he speaks, you hear the careful words and soothing rhythms of a well-trained scholar. When he gestures, you see the firm hands and long fingers of a talented woodwright. He began by describing how he came to know Walker Percy.*

What I provided Walker, in part, was a connection to youth, to what the younger generation was doing. I met Walker when he was a participant in the Community Relations Council in Covington. The council's job was really to try and do something before the more militant groups came into Covington to create trouble, is the way it was looked at. Actually, it turned out, whether by design or not, to be somewhat effective. There were not a lot of—there were some cross burnings and such, but there were no really heavy, angry demonstrations in Covington. Some progress was made there. But that's how I came to know Walker.

*You must have been a good bit younger than Walker.*

Well, I'm approaching sixty-six, Walker would be approaching eighty, so I was fifteen years or so younger. I knew of him before, in the early sixties, but not very well. Once we were thrown together in these community groups, then I got to know him better. It was around that same time that we started the discussion group. We actually called it the "Great Books Group," and we put together some of the membership. We moved from house to house every two weeks, and the group is still going on, it's been nearly thirty years. Bunt dropped out. She continued in the group for quite a while in the years following Walker's death. I think she's grown tired of living in the shadow of Walker. I don't mean that to sound bad—she's just got to move on with her life. She was always gracious. I've known her as long as I've known Walker, but you can tell that she must wonder, "When will this shadow behind me let me be alone, let me be who I am?"

*So when you got to know Walker, were you acting as president of the Seminary College [St. Joseph Seminary College at the Abbey in Covington]?*

When I first met Walker, I had just finished graduate school at Tulane and I was the dean of students at the Abbey's college. Within a few years, I became president of the college. All during that time, my contact with Walker accelerated. But most of my contact with Walker came from the discussion group and the community meetings. For a while I was interim chaplain at St. Paul's High School in Covington, and I would go there on Sundays for Mass. Walker and Bunt would walk over from their house to attend, and I'd see them afterward and chat with them. Sometimes we would go back to their place—Walker often had other people there.

Sunday afternoon was kind of a meeting time for people that he wanted to see or who wanted to see him. You'd meet some interesting people there.

*What was Walker's affiliation with the Abbey prior to your being there?*

Curiosity. He would occasionally come out for Sunday Mass because I think he liked the atmosphere, the liturgy, the music, the sort of lifestyle that was there. I think he was curious about that. He knew a number of people there, some of the members there.

*From reading what you said to Jay Tolson, it's inferred that Percy was not very comfortable talking about trivia and ordinary things. You said something to the effect that he always wanted to talk about "life or death" matters.*

He was not one for just sitting down and talking about football games, or the weather, or to ask how your golf game was—never. I never had a conversation with Walker over stuff you would talk to your coworkers or colleagues about. There was something about him. He was scratching already—he would squirm if you weren't into something that was making him think, or where he could get some kind of insight into something, or where there were some opinions being expressed. He liked to talk content, or ideas, or reactions, or what you were feeling. He wanted to hear it from you. He didn't want to tell you a lot about what he was thinking; he wanted you to tell him what you were thinking.

*Do you think he was that way with most folks?*

Yeah, a lot of people. I think he played around at some things; his lunch group would sort of spar over political jokes and this kind of thing, but I think he really wanted to evoke from whoever he was talking to some manifestation of what makes you tick.

*Do you think that was intellectual curiosity or some type of emotional need that he had?*

I think it was genuine, intellectual curiosity. He was not really a spontaneously personable person, in the sense of someone who might be easily outgoing and glad to see you. In fact, he would just kind of move off if he didn't know you. I tell one—I've said this a bunch of times—I tell an anecdote about a person who wrote me a letter in the early seventies, a lady from Lafayette who was with a garden club or a woman's auxiliary club or something, and they were doing a cookbook. Somebody gave them my name as a friend of Walker Percy's, so she writes me a letter and asks me to get Walker to write an introduction to their cookbook. Well, I wrote her back a little note that read politely, "I'm sorry, I'm not Walker's literary agent, and I don't do this kind of thing. We're friends."

I showed the letter to Walker as a kind of goad. I said, "See, I don't bother you with this kind of thing." His response to me was really quick; he said, "That's one of the reasons why I like you. You never traded on that kind of thing." He was real quick to point that out. It's an indication that he did not like not only the trivialities of conversation, but he didn't want these trivial connections. He did not want an entrée to that through his friends. He didn't want to be used in some way.

*So to quote Mrs. Percy, when Walker wanted so much to belong to a community, that didn't mean that he wanted to stand on a street corner and jaw. What do you think she meant by that?*

He didn't mind doing that with kind of blue-collar folks. He made his daily walk to the post office and would collect his mail, and he knew so-and-so, or he would pass Tuggie's Bar. He kept contact with the "little people" on a casual basis, but he did not linger long, talking. He did the right strokes, to remember your name, tell you hello in his familiar routines. I'm sure he didn't mind chatting if a plumber came out to the house; he was curious about that. But he was always looking for material. Those people were not likely to try to get something out of him other than to get paid for their work or something. This was just ordinary human contact, and I think that was okay with him. He was not a sparkling, outgoing personality. He had a good sense of humor, but he was not terribly spontaneous.

*That's interesting considering how strongly his sense of humor comes out in his books. Speaking of gathering material, in your reading of his works, did you ever recognize yourself or a familiar situation?*

No, I never thought of myself in connection with his books. I recognized a lot of things. He'd call me three, four, five, or six times during a book he was working on. I remember one occasion when he wanted to know what the model of a Chevrolet car was—he didn't quite know the name of this car, but he wanted to use the right term. It was an Impala or something. I remember telling him that he had the name for PVC pipe wrong in the book where the main character was going to burn down the mansion, called . . .

*"Lancelot"?*

Yes, in *Lancelot* he had some of the materials wrong. He had actually gone to Smith Hardware, trying to get the materials right. He would ask you questions like that, if he knew you were somebody who might know that. He knew of my interests, that I did a lot of mechanical work, electrical work, like that, somebody who was some kind of pseudo-intellectual who could work with his hands, so he would ask questions about those activities.

*I remember thinking of what Walker had written about his uncle, Will Percy, that he was "too much in the wintry kingdom of the mind" and not enough a part of the community. I am thinking that this sounds accurate about Walker too, but he kind of takes that away with his novels and makes you think otherwise, hearing what you've had to say.*

I think he liked the contact with the little people, I really do. I think he felt comfortable that way. He drove around in a pickup truck, and he sort of liked that image because it made him fit, like the people who belonged here, the original denizens of St. Tammany Parish, the more redneck kind of folks. I think he liked that.

*Why?*

Because I think—I don't know the answer to that, but I suspect that he found the work of his craft so taxing that it kept him tight all the time. He was not somebody who wrote spontaneously; he was somebody who wrote laboriously, and he revised, went back and changed, and at the same time I think he wanted it to be art. He had to make it art, it didn't flow out of him. If you read an Updike novel, you somehow feel that John Updike is painting a picture; his words are coming out just like paints on a canvas, and you get this beautiful image and style. There is no question about John Updike being an artist. But with Walker, he had this huge, philosophical overlay for everything that he did. He was still fighting philosophical problems that people were yawning over in his era. My God, Descartes—who's still fighting over Descartes? He was still fighting the old issues of linguistic analysis. Walker wanted to kind of bring this stuff forward, embed it in art, tell a good story. He wanted the applause, he wanted the acclaim, but he didn't want to do all the stooping, all the public relations that you had to do to win that. I think that was very taxing for him. And his relief, in one sense, was to get into a pickup truck and kind of fade into the piney woods, not the redneck culture, but sort of being faceless, being a part of that, and to hear everyday stories. Why did Walker sit in front of a TV? I suspect that he was sampling popular culture. I don't know all his hours of viewing, but he would watch these senseless kind of sitcoms and stuff like that.

*There are allusions to "Oprah," "Phil Donahue," and other TV shows in some of his works, sure, especially in "Lost in the Cosmos."*

He used to tell us he watched all that. He didn't apologize for it. Stuff that I didn't even know what he was talking about, but he would watch these things, and I think it was the same—that he was trying to stay connected in what was going on in the world and in the country. All of that was true. But also I think he was also trying to bail out of this heavy pressure of being an artist, a philosopher. He was trying to write stories that talk about big questions. That's really what I've always liked about Walker's writing. It isn't just a story that he's telling. He's getting into the real issues. What is the meaning of life? How do people get through a Tuesday afternoon?

What else is there to do on a Sunday but go to church? Why do you go, what is happening? What makes people tick? Why do you bother to get up in the morning? Why do you bother to go the speed limit? Why do you bother to go to work? He wanted to know all that.

*So the community connections we've discussed, they were his way of coming back down into the street and blinking in the sunlight?*

Yes.

*Many priests and ministers develop a sort of personal, shorthand reference system for the types of parishioners they deal with— wanderer, seeker, crusader, etc. Having been behind the pulpit, what sort of classifications did you make of those who came to you? How did you see Walker?*

A wanderer, no question. A sovereign wayfarer. I want to say this gently: Walker was lost in the sense that he saw so much ambivalence. Not just "lost in the cosmos," but he—I guess this brings together a bunch of opinions I have about Walker that I don't mean in terms of criticism, just in terms of observation. I don't think Walker was ever comfortable as a Catholic. He was not really, completely Catholic. Walker was still Protestant, but he saw through the kind of thin veil that you find in Protestantism, and he saw the richness of the Catholic church, but he also saw through the pomp and circumstance that was there that didn't compute to any more exceptional meaning than did the overly individualistic Protestant ethic and its peculiar conflicts. I think he had these conflicts all along. He was searching. Just like philosophy, he was trying to bring ideas that he liked or that he wrestled with into a more contemporary setting and apply them to human beings and see why they tick. He chose the novel form, but I think he'd rather have written a book on philosophy if he could ever get his ideas settled. He was always looking for something; he was a Will Barrett or Thomas Moore character. I think he saw himself as a want-to-be champion of Truth and Right and Direction and Meaning, but he was skeptical about all of these. This notion of the malaise being perched on your shoulder, always there—Walker was trying to swat that off all his life. I don't think he ever found something that was completely convincing for him. He just kept peeling the onion, trying to move further and further to the core of something, and I don't think he ever got there. The great philosophical issues, the big questions, never go away.

*So do you think he was troubled with his "search," or did he become comfortable with it?*

I think it bothered him. He brought some baggage from his family that his biographers have talked about, and I think he worried a lot about his wife and his children and their needs and how this coincided with a lot of his misgivings and philosophical meanderings and wanderings. I just think that he never looked comfortable. He never looked like he was completely relaxed or that he had paid his dues, made his peace, and mellowed out in life. In his latter years with the discussion group, within the last four or five years, and there was the beginning of his cancer. He eased off a bit. He wasn't as squirming or questioning, but I think that some of that had to do with how physically he was at a lower performance level. But at the discussion groups, he'd always pounce back. What is going on here? What is the author trying to say? What is the message? Those were always his questions.

*There's been discussion of Walker's fights with depression. Based on what you've said, though, do you see Walker as being more filled with anxiety than the "malaise"?*

Yes, I think he was always very anxious, very tense. He was moody, but then anybody gets moody when you're trying to hatch something. He was always trying to write something. He was not satisfied with his writing and continued to revise it. At the same time the demands of everyday life—pay the bills, take care of this, go pick up the mail, take telephone calls, on and on—that created a tension. I don't think it was depression as much as it was just being tense. He was appointed by the governor to an LSU board to try and improve higher education or something. He went to two meetings, and he was telling me about them. He said, "I sat next to ex-Governor McKeithen, and all the man wanted to do was tell jokes. I wanted to get on with the business, and I couldn't stand it, so I quit. I resigned." He just walked away from it. I could picture him right there at the meeting, saying something like, "Come on guys, what are we here for? Are we going to improve higher education?" and being tense the entire time. And McKeithen, being absolutely, utterly relaxed, retired, now the ex-governor, trying to feed them jokes. There was no way Walker could do that.

*It's interesting how much of what you say can be seen between Shelby Foote and Percy in their correspondence.*

I never knew Shelby. I spotted him a couple of times. I got to know him better through the Civil War commentary, where I got a whole different image of him. He comes across, not only vocally, but in his persona, as being self-contained, relaxed, and easy. He could probably toss stuff off that Walker couldn't, that Walker would brood over. I think they were two very different people. I think Walker was always fraught with tension.

*You mentioned earlier that part of what you provided Walker was a "connection to youth." What do you think he was looking for there?*

I think he wanted to know what was happening with the upcoming generation. I think he was generally interested in that, not just jousting with dead philosophers and his publishers. He wanted to know what was happening, and I think, as the whole civil rights movement and the youth culture had surfaced, it caught him like it caught most of us. The cultural changes went a lot further than he thought. When you get into a movement like this where you're breaking down barriers, getting rid of some of the courtesies and the established etiquette, it becomes fascinating. I have to admit that even when I was in graduate school in 1964–65, if somebody came in in just a pair of shorts and barefoot and put their feet up on a table, no shirt, nothing, at a university, I was kind of stunned. Walker found this movement of youth and the shift in mores compelling. I think he was curious about it all. He always claimed that he wanted to teach freshman English, and he offered to me many times to teach courses at the college, but he never delivered on that. I told him carte blanche, any time you want to do that, it's fine. He did teach a number of times at Loyola. He didn't want to fool with the graduate students. He already had worked with his own novels, and he didn't want to do a lot of copy reading. He wanted to hear people's creative ideas, so he was interested in younger people and what they were thinking about. He was interested in spontaneity because he wasn't terribly spontaneous. I think he was a somewhat boring lecturer. In talking, he was not easy in front of an audience. If he had a prepared script, he would be extremely witty and kind of devastating with his comments, when he was prepared. But in front of a class, where he was describing the writer's process and such things, he had difficulty. He preferred hearing from them and reading their papers. He didn't teach often. I think he wanted to do it more, but he didn't want to get drawn into people using him or somehow getting involved in the bureaucracy of college. He could have taught anywhere he wanted. I have to go back to his tension. I think when he did something like that, it was a relief for a while, but then it began to be another form of tension or obligation or worry.

*In your interaction with Walker, was your relationship to him in any way that of a priest or a psychologist? Do you think, as has been suggested, that he was seeking to make you his spiritual adviser?*

I never liked my relationship with Walker in terms of me being a clergyman and Walker being a parishioner. That wasn't of interest to me, though I did wind up performing the marriage for his daughter Ann as a favor to Walker. I never thought of Walker that way, though I think he tried to build some sort of connection because of my clerical position. I remember very clearly, now that you mention it, that he called me one evening at eight o'clock while I was still in my office at the Abbey's college. He said he had to come over and talk to me, and I told him sure, any time. We hung up, and I figured he was coming, then he phoned again. He said again, "I've got to come over and talk to you. I am going to come." A half hour later he drives up in his pickup, I meet him out front, and he walks in. He was talking about something he was mad about at first, and I asked him to share whatever it was he needed to see me about. We sat down for only a few minutes, then he said, "Well, thank you," and he left the office. It was not a meeting, and I wasn't bringing him any type of religious comfort. I was just anybody. He had to get out, I think, move around. He had to get out of where he was mentally, go someplace. Whether he saw something en route or got some kind of connection in his head, I was just a person that he knew, and it had nothing to do with a ministerial function at all.

*Sounds like something he mentioned in "Lost in the Cosmos," about the different ways that an author has to try and gain re-entry after writing. Do you think that his behavior suggests a manic state?*

Not really. There were times when you could see some of that sort of thing in Walker, but I don't know for a fact that it was true of him. I'm acquainted with bipolar disorders; I've worked with a number of young people who've had problems with manic depression.

*Did you remain friends after you left the Abbey?*

We remained friendly, but I was not in his intimate circle of people who he saw every Tuesday and Wednesday or golfed with. I was too busy, and I didn't invade his routine. I rarely ever called Walker. The initiation was from his end. I never tried to see him or ask him to do something, other than our scheduled meetings with the discussion group. We had an exchange of letters for some time about him needing someone to talk over religious matters with. I told him quite candidly in a letter that I didn't feel competent to do that but that I was willing to discuss whatever he'd like to talk about. He wrote back and said that he'd take that as a qualified yes. Then I talked to him on the phone and said, "I'm willing to reflect on whatever you want to talk about. I'm not intimidated by this, you don't scare me. I don't feel that I'm competent to answer the questions that you want answered, but I'm certainly interested in them." So we had some contact after that, but it was always in his strange way. He would call you, ask you what you think about this, what you think about that. He'd always show his nervous ticks — scratching movements, fidgets. It was not that he was uncomfortable with you when he'd do that. He was uncomfortable with what he was thinking about. He had no reason to be uncomfortable with me. I think there was a trust. I was not uncomfortable with him other than saying, "Good grief, I can't answer these big questions. I can't bail you out of this, but I'm willing to explore."

*You seem to be comfortable with the search and lack of answers.*

I've made my peace a long time ago with life being ambivalent. If you can't live with ambiguity—well, you've got to.

One of the things that I might pass on is that I thought early on that Walker was a lot more liberal and open-minded than he really was. My first encounter with him was around the work for civil rights. I didn't know a lot about his Uncle Will; I didn't know a lot about his real background. I only read *Lanterns on the Levee* some time after that. I didn't understand Walker's biography. I only knew that he was a writer and a recluse. Here he was all of a sudden wanting to do good things with civil rights for humanity and the community. I always kind of stuck with that, and I think he was open-minded, but I don't think he was completely open in terms of changing conduct. I think he was a little hesitant when it got down to being involved in a demonstration. He would do things quietly, but he did not want to get overtly involved in a lot of stuff. I was surprised with the idealism with which he defended the Catholic church—I thought unnecessarily in some ways. He agreed to be on a papal commission and went to Rome once. I told him he was nuts to go to that, that it was a put-up job, that they were trying to use his prestige as a writer and a so-called Catholic author to just do a job on women, and that the church was not going to change any of these kind of things. I think I kind of ruffled his feathers a bit about that. He was more tolerant of the pomp and circumstance of the church because I think he saw the Catholic church as still something that carried the torch for a code of conduct for people to follow in their lives, even though he himself was uncomfortable with some of the specific requirements. Yet he ideally thought that having this symbol of the pope, and a uniform doctrine, was the benefit of the church. I tried to explain to him that this code of conduct isn't uniformly observed by the church hierarchy or everyday Catholics. Pedophile clergy, alcoholism, and depression are aggravated by church structures, rules, clerical culture, the devaluation of women, politics of annulments —these things make the "code" a pastoral quagmire. Walker was interested in but not terribly enamored of getting into those kind of things.

*Do you think he regarded the Catholic church in light of the chivalric code?*

He admired that. He still admired that kind of thing. Just like with Ronald Reagan. I think he admired Reagan's simplification, Reagan's communication of what we all should hold to. But I think he had doubts, serious doubts, about a lot of that kind of stuff, yet he kind of wanted that code. He was not as liberal as I was, and I was very careful in trying not to foist on him things that would tear down his beliefs. He was more insightful than I was on a lot of things; he was ahead of me on some things.

*It sounds as if he had invested a great deal of personal stability in the Catholic faith.*

That's still a mystery to me. I have never considered Walker a complete Catholic—certainly not a pious or Mediterranean Catholic. One of the biggest jokes in my life was at his funeral, when two archbishops had come to the Abbey for his funeral and they talked about Walker Percy, and I suspect that neither one of them had ever read one of his books. And yet this was a "Catholic author." He was no more a Catholic author than I'm a Catholic author. He simply appreciated the symbolic value and the historical richness of the Catholic church.

*Another question: You were speaking of John Updike and how some of his images were like paintings. Do you remember any places in Percy's books that did that?*

I haven't read Walker's stuff in a long time, so don't hold me to an exegesis of his work. I think they all kind of fall together. But one of the ones that I liked was *The Second Coming*, where Will Barrett discovers the wood nymph and lowers the stove down into the cave. I think Walker really enjoyed writing that kind of thing—all the ropes and pulleys. It was almost lyrical, finding this wood nymph, this discovery. Of course, that's a bit of autobiographical fantasy, to be able to tromp through the woods and discover this strange, exotic little lady. I think Walker relished that, and I think he relished writing that. I think some of the critics beat up on him for some of that, as I recall, but I told him, "Walker, I thought you were really getting on to something there. I really enjoyed it," and I still do.

I don't think of Walker in terms of trying to compete with John Updike. I think of Walker more as trying to compete with Saul Bellow. If you want my favorite author in all the world, it's Saul Bellow. What Bellow is talking about is what's going on in the head of the person that is the voice. What the voice is interpreting is the head of the person he's interacting with. Frankly, I don't think Walker did it as well as Saul Bellow. I think that Saul Bellow's ability to do this exceeded Walker's. However, where Saul played with philosophical ideas, Walker was much more serious about what he was trying to write, though at times he was humorous and satirical.

Saul is more absurd, he's released. He just lets this stuff come out. These incredible observations are going on in the heads of these people, and it's all with a kind of masterful ease. Walker is tortured. He's trying to shove his ideas or his concerns or his thoughts into these characters in these pages while he's still trying to write a good story. He set a much more difficult agenda for himself and his novels than Bellow did.

*What did I not ask you about Percy? What else needs to be said?*

People have asked me all kinds of things about Walker—his relationships with women, his so-called girlfriend and lovers, what he believed about the church, whether he was really a good writer. I've been asked just about everything I can think of. I guess one of the observations I've had is that Walker always wanted to be more successful than he was, but an ambivalence comes in. He wanted to write about serious epistemological issues. I think that he was stunned at the sort of cult following that he had, that people saw in his work far more than he himself put in his work, even though he was trying to put in his work all these philosophical quandaries that he was continuing to balance in his mind all the time. If you didn't see him as this kind of complicated person—he wanted to be an artist, he wanted to be a philosopher, he wanted to be part of a community, he wanted to be a recluse, he wanted to be southern because being southern had not only a historical connection, but it had a kind of cachet. He liked that southern pose. He *was* southern.

*Though he seemed to deny that he was a southern author every time it came up.*

I would still rather be called southern than northern. *I* like that. There's something to it.

*Regarding his relationship to the South, what do you think of the progress he made before his illness? Does it seem to you that his move—from Mississippi to North Carolina for college, then to New York for medical school, and finally his return from the sanitorium in New York to the South, but to Louisiana instead of Mississippi— are those the steps of a young man in a love/hate relationship with the South?*

Yes. You need only go back to the *Esquire* article ["Bourbon"] to see where he loved trading on his southern charm, writing about bourbon. He relished that kind of thing in his lighter moments, if there really ever were very many light moments with Walker.

*It could be suggested, then, that he went to New York thinking to find an answer to the problems he had encountered while growing up in the South?*

That's where the intellectual elite are supposed to be. I think he wanted to test that and draw on it, sure.

# Nikki Barringer, Attorney
COVINGTON, LOUISIANA

*Nikki Barringer, a local attorney and close friend of Walker Percy's, spoke of the author from the living room of the home on Jahncke Avenue where he had been Percy's neighbor. The house is easy to miss. The yard is heavily wooded, allowing for a large measure of peace and privacy. Barringer, the Percys, and other friends used to meet in the same living room, its walls lined with bookshelves holding many books, for literary discussions and social occasions.*

Walker first moved to Covington when I was still in college. He was very much involved with philosophy in those days, although he never had any formal philosophical training. He came to the interest in philosophy later on in his life. He knew that I was a philosophy major at Yale, and he would try to nail down whatever formal stuff I was studying up there. As it happened, I was reading Suzanne Langer and a lot of the people that he became very deeply involved with. I was taking a course called "Symbolism and Experience," which I didn't understand for sour apples. I still have only the most vague grasp of what Walker is talking about in all those essays that deal with that particular branch of things. But as a result of that, he showed me a lot of the early drafts of his essays that were subsequently published in philosophical journals. We talked about those things in great depth.

After I graduated from law school in 1960 at Tulane, I went into practice with my father. After about a year, in about 1961 or 1962, I moved into this house with my wife, Millie Slater Barringer. We lived here for quite a number of years—about twenty years. We were next-door neighbors with the Percys. Once or twice a week, we would walk down there and have sundown drinks with them, or they would walk down here and have sundown drinks with us. We were very close.

Walker started the Great Books discussion group that we had here, which I attended with him every two weeks. Most of our meetings were held here in the house. From time to time I represented him as a lawyer, but he was never involved in any great amount of litigation. I mainly conferred with him on a number of things from time to time. We were very close friends with Walker and Bunt, and Millie taught Mary Pratt in school. Millie was teaching at St. Scholastica while she was getting her Ph.D. in theater.

*I have the impression from my reading that you were one of his closest friends.*

That accolade would have to go to Shelby [Foote]. I never knew Shelby. In those days, nobody even knew who he was. He would drift through town once every few years, but I never had the occasion to meet him. He was also very close with his brothers. I wouldn't say that I was Walker's closest friend, but we were probably as close as almost anybody in Covington. Walker had a number of different coteries of friends that didn't really mix very much. There was the book group, one of which I was, and there was the philosophy group, one of which I was. Then he had his Catholic friends, one of whom I wasn't, and that consisted of people like Chink Baldwin, and the Wards, and the Reeds, and the Crosses, and while I knew these people, we weren't very close. Then he had a luncheon group he hung out with—Bob Milling, Rhoda Faust, and some others later on were part of that little enclave. Lynn Hill was part of that. While I know all these people, the thing that we have mainly in common is the fact that we shared an affection for Walker.

*Could you comment on how he fit himself into the community of Covington? I've read and heard descriptions from "recluse" to "average fellow around town."*

The myth that Walker was a recluse is just exactly that. He was not a reclusive person. He was a genial, sweet, loving man, and just about anybody could approach Walker and talk to him about something that they were mutually interested in. All those books of conversations with Walker Percy, there are two of them, are excellent examples of how well he interacted with strangers. You'd never find that sort of thing kicking around in the closet of J. D. Salinger. Now there's a guy who's a recluse. Walker was anything but that. He was vitally interested in affairs of the day. He did a lot of work with the Head Start program, which brought him into contact with many people, all up and down the social scale.

When we started the Head Start group—he was one of the initiators of it, and ours was one of the first Head Start programs anywhere—in those days, it was required by the government that the people who manage the organization must stay in close touch with the consumers, the parents of the children. In those early days of Head Start, it was necessary that your application include all kinds of information about your community. We all looked at this and were really at our wit's end about it and thought that we'd have to scrounge up all these statistics, and it was a hard-assed job. It never occurred to us at first to call upon the parents to help out with the assembly of all this information, but we very rapidly learned, very much to our amazement, that they could do it better and more accurately than we could. So in the process of putting together these applications, we had occasion to get very close to many of the parents who were involved in the Head Start program, and Walker was just as amiable and able to do that as any of the rest of us, and he even drove the school bus for a year or so and very much enjoyed doing that. This is not the picture of a man who is a recluse. Anybody who tries to tell you that just doesn't know what they're talking about, it's that simple. Now he was not a guy to suffer fools with any great spirit of gladness, and he was jealous of his time, and he didn't like people butting into his life who didn't know what he was working on or who didn't have any common interests with him, but he was one of the most generous people with his time, for people who did, that I know of.

*Would you comment on Walker's involvement with the civil rights movement in this area?*

We had a major flap over the Confederate flag. Louis Wagner, the late Louis Wagner, bless his memory, had one in his office. He was principal of the local high school in those days, and he was a fellow churchman of mine. He and his wife went to the Episcopal church. This was in the days when the Confederate flag as a symbol was just beginning to be identified with the Klan and all that. It was the kind of thing then that I never would have given a second thought to. I'm sort of sensitive to that sort of thing, but it just never occurred to me that anybody would make a big to-do about it. Well, they integrated the school, and the black kids, as they were then called—"African American" had not caught on as a cognomen at that point—were incensed about it. There were a bunch of them that raised hell. They brought a lawsuit over it, and Walker actually testified in the lawsuit. I have the testimony that he gave somewhere, and I was going to write an article for *Harper's* about it.

*What was the nature of the testimony?*

Well, actually, it was rather dull testimony. I went to great lengths to dig it out of the record; they were stored in Texas, and I was hoping that they would be deathless words of Walker Percy that would make good publication, but actually it's very dull. It's about 12–13 pages of transcript. What Walker did was simply to testify that he was a person knowledgeable in the business of icons in the United States and what was going on, and that he was a writer, and that yes, indeed, this kind of thing would incite children in the school to aggressive behavior, stir them up. Actually, the black kids were extremely well-behaved. There was going to be a march about it one day, but it rained and the march got canceled. The court decided the case in favor of our side and made Louis Wagner take the flag out of his office.

But we had some other pretty ugly incidents that happened in those days. Once we had what was called the Mardi Gras Riot, where some rather ebullient folks after a Mardi Gras Day parade were in the black section of town and a lady got shot. I represented her, sued against the kid who she said had shot her. It was probably about half accident and half nastiness, and the court felt that we had not adequately proven that this was the kid who had shot her. But it was felt by a number of people, following the Kennedy assassinations and the death of Martin Luther King, that all the seeds that were possible for a genuine riot were brewing around here. There was a series of frictional problems. What we did was to get together a group of people who had met each other in the Head Start effort, and we put together a biracial group that consisted of Helen and Leroy Frick, Walker, myself, and others. We began to get together about once or twice a month and just talk over problems that were occurring to see what we could do about them. As a result of the very quiet efforts and pleasant cajolery and diplomatic goodwill exercised by this biracial group, we were able to head off any real serious friction. Things went pretty well in this end of the parish. There were other places in St. Tammany Parish where this was not true. Down around the Pearl River is a stronghold of the Klan, and things got pretty ugly down there. There were some church bombings.

*How long was this committee in effect?*

To call it a committee makes it sound rather more official than it was. It was just a group of people who got together, who were available to other people, and they knew if there was a problem, they could get hold of one of us and talk it over. We also had the problem of the march through Satsuma. This was a group of black people who were marching on the state capital, and there's a little town called Satsuma on the other side of Hammond. They camped at Satsuma one night, and the Klan was going to attack them. The Deacons for Defense were ready for them and whipped the shit out of the Klan, and all of the marchers got run into the parish jail. I and a number of other lawyers went up and got them sprung. The court did the right thing, certainly, to let them go. The little town of Satsuma was completely flattened by the construction of Interstate 12. That part of the state tends to be sort of rife with Klansmen. One of the civilizing influences up there has been that the Klan has generally lost size by ethnicity. There are a great many Italians that have moved into those parishes, and they've sort of diluted the population to the extent that the Klan is not really much of a force up there anymore. That's my impression.

*Did Percy participate at all in the country club set here?*

I don't think he ever frequented the country club. He and Bunt went through a phase where they played golf for a while, and he may have played out there some, but he preferred to do his active socializing either in the homes of friends or in his own home. Walker worked very hard. He didn't have time to putter around.

*So where do you think Percy stood in the social strata here?*

Well, everybody has their own circle of friends. I never thought of it as being stratified particularly. Anybody around here can hang out with anybody else. To be quite frank with you, the one time I was ever made aware of the fact that there were color lines or barriers existent was one night when I was driving home. I drove down Tyler Street to get to the Folsom Highway, and a cop stopped me and told me to get out of this part of town. He said, "You don't belong here." It never occurred to me that there was a part of town I couldn't go into. Our family was always very broad-minded with regard to matters of race, almost in a sort of militant way. The big battle over the schools here when I was growing up was over busing, but a different kind of busing. The black rural students were not given the benefit of a school bus to get them to school. The result was that the children of the people who worked for us were brought to school every day by my father, along with me. My mother got along with the school superintendent in a reasonably amicable way, but they had many a fight over that particular issue. Eventually, school buses were put in for blacks, but the battle to get that busing was a big battle. It was one of the chief areas where "separate but equal" as a myth became completely obvious. If you're not affording school buses to a whole segment of the population, what kind of "separate but equal" was that?

One thing that Covington does not have, I think, is the kind of stratification among the blacks that you find in New Orleans. New Orleans had this very strict rule that if you were darker than a brown bag, you just didn't hang out with anybody who was lighter than a brown bag. It was called the "brown bag rule," and they used the brown bag from the A&P store as the official King's Foot, the litmus paper test, as it were.

It never occurred to me to even ask the question about social strata. It came as a great shock to me at one of those biracial meetings when one of the blacks said that I was part of the power structure around here. I said, "What power structure? Me?" It never occurred to me that I had any power. I always considered myself an outsider at just about everything.

*When you first started talking to him about philosophy, would you have guessed that he would have the kind of international reputation that he has now? I asked Mrs. Percy that question, and she said she knew it would happen.*

I think that Walker's reputation as a writer generally snuck up on all of us.

*Was Walker surprised?*

I think so. I don't think that Walker ever thought that he was going to be world-famous until it actually happened. The thing that really caused the avalanche to start was the incident with A. J. Liebling. He had come down here to do an article about Earl Long when

Earl Long was put into a mental institution down here. I think it was on that trip that Liebling picked up a copy of *The Moviegoer*, which Knopf was not pushing. Knopf was almost embarrassed by *The Moviegoer*. They just never did anything for that book. Liebling sent the book to his wife, who was on the commission for the National Book Award that year, and she promoted it to the NBA. It was at that point that Walker's star really began to ascend.

Now the reputation as being a person interested in semiotics came a lot later than that and accreted grain by grain. He always said that he was an amateur in that area. If you read the letters to Kenneth Ketner, this is emphasized repeatedly. Now Ketner and I carry on a fairly brisk correspondence from time to time. Have you read Ketner's biography of Charles Sanders Peirce?

*No, I haven't.*

Well, the title of the book is *His Glass Essence*, and it's a very interesting book. I commend it as necessary collateral reading to studying this aspect of Walker's work. Walker's relationship to Ketner was very fruitful for both of them. It just so happens that Ketner adored Walker's work, and he is certainly one of the leading scholars of Peirce. I studied under Paul Weiss at Yale but did not deal with Peirce very much, but Weiss is also the other leading exponent of Peirce.

It's characteristic that the letters between Walker and Ketner are called *A Thief of Peirce*. What Walker was doing, and always allowed as how he was doing it, was taking little bits here and there from the Peirce canon and putting it together in his own way. As a matter of fact, I'm not sure whether Walker ever realized himself to what extent the triadic aspects of the Delta Factor, as they're reflected in Peirce, are inimical to the whole idea of Roman Catholicism. The fact of the matter is that you cannot build a dogmatic system of religion within the Peirce structure. They are as inimical to one another as the Ptolemaic Universe is to the notions of Copernicus and Galileo. They just don't mesh. It took me a long time to realize that. I read the Ketner letters, and then I read the Peirce bio, and suddenly it dawned on me, and I wondered, "Walker, what were you doing getting all this interested in CSP? It's simply not going to fit with Roman Catholicism." And that may have been what he was referring to in that rather pithy quotation that comes from the letters where he says that he's stealing from Peirce what he wants and leaving the rest behind.

*Did Walker talk to you about his conversion to Catholicism?*

Well, yes, not his conversion, specifically, but we discussed religion on any number of occasions. My mother and I are old Theosophists, so obviously we are in a different system than Walker. But I was able to talk knowledgeably about Catholicism because I went to St. Paul's and graduated from St. Paul's in 1952, and so I'd had seven years of indoctrination in the religion of Catholicism at the hands of the Christian Brothers. So I knew a lot about Catholicism, more probably than my mother did, and Walker talked to my mother a lot about Theosophy, probably more than he did with me. We would discuss those things, but never at the level of discussing Walker's own personal religious journey. When he was made a papal legate of some sort, appointed by the Pope to an advisory council, I urged him to go over there and tell the Pope a few things about what the mainstream of American Catholicism was saying, thinking, and doing, and he told me in no uncertain terms to back off, and I did.

*What had you recommended that he say?*

I recommended that he let the Pope know, for example, that the church's line on birth control is simply not going to continue to fly in the United States. And I have Catholic friends in New York who are very gung ho in the woman's movement over the right to choose in the abortion controversy, and I suggested that perhaps His Holiness ought to realize that there's trouble on the horizon there. These were not things that Walker was really gung ho about particularly, and it certainly never appeared in his work as being a focus until *The Thanatos Syndrome*.

I have one little nugget to share related to *The Thanatos Syndrome*. Walker, after every book that he wrote, used to say "I've written my last novel." Bunt and I and Millie [and Walker] were driving into New Orleans one night, and we were going to see *Das Boot*, the German submarine movie, and partly as a result of that trip, *The Thanatos Syndrome* came to be written. Walker started reminiscing about his Wanderjahr in Germany, and in the best passages in *The Thanatos Syndrome*, all the Father Smith confession sequence, which I think most scholars agree is the kernel of the book, Walker was talking about his perception of Germany in those days. He had also said, earlier in the evening, that he wasn't going to write any more books. I said to that and his talk about his Wanderjahr that I think for one of the leading novelists of our century who has had that experience not to write about it is a dreadful omission. And he said, "Look. Everybody that tries to write about the Nazi scourge, everybody that tries to tackle it—it's something that you just can't write about. It's too big, it's too nasty, too ugly, and you either get bogged down in maudlin sentimentality or it just doesn't work." He cited Kurt Vonnegut's situation and Norman Mailer, and he said that it just doesn't work. I told him that "somebody has to bear witness to these things, and for you, having the bully pulpit of the American reading public's eye, to overlook doing something about it would, I think, be a very grave oversight." And the result of all that was *The Thanatos Syndrome*, which most people, I think, regard as his least successful book, and I kind of do too, except for the Father Smith confession sequence. It certainly is the central idea of the book, and the whole idea of life, of the sacredness of life from the Roman Catholic point of view, is obviously central to it. But I never heard him get particularly exercised over the abortion issue early on.

*What did he have to say about Vonnegut's work? I assume he was talking about "Slaughterhouse V"?*

Not a lot. He just mentioned that it was one of the books that dealt with the Nazis, but I think he said that Vonnegut did better with it than most people did because he approached the matter obliquely, and that was the only way you could deal with it. You couldn't confront the matter head on. It would be interesting to see what he would have done with *Schindler's List* and how he would have responded to that since the Holocaust was certainly dealt with in that film as directly as anything that I know of, and it certainly seemed to be successful.

*Do you remember anything else that he said about his travels in Germany?*

I remember that he had the notion that it could have been anybody who went over that cliff, that the Germans were not all bad people, that they were very decent people for the most part. He had difficulty understanding how the whole thing became so horribly brutal and nasty and terrible, and how they got swept into it. And of course he deals with that more articulately, and at much greater length, in *The Thanatos Syndrome*. I believe he may have mentioned his cousin, who was this wonderfully shining youth who appears in this book with the bayonet and who goes off to the young knight's swearing in. It sounds like a kind of Teutonic Ku Klux Klan meeting.

I don't know why he got the doldrums every time he finished a book. It was like postpartum depression. Apparently a lot of writers feel that way. I don't—I get very ebullient when I finish something. I'm working on a novel now.

*What exactly are you working on?*

My book is a story about my life with my father, who was a lawyer. My father contracted—succumbed to—Alzheimer's disease, and he went from practicing law and being a very highly regarded, very smart, intellectual man to not being able to tie his shoelaces in a period of about six months. He was one of the real depth-charged Alzheimer's patients. As we grow older, it's becoming recognized that more and more people who were simply thought of as senile were actually suffering from Alzheimer's disease.

Dad's situation was a little bit uncharacteristic in that he took a sudden plunge. My book interweaves that whole story of my father's descent into Alzheimer's and into madness—what happened to him was that they did some medical procedures on him which actually kicked him over the edge, I think, and probably did some stuff upstairs that shouldn't have happened. They gave him a pneumo-encephalogram, which was a disaster, and he went from being a kind of pleasant and happy but rather dotty old man to suddenly becoming the last few pages of *King Lear*.

So the book weaves that part of the story together with some of the theories of Theosophy about reincarnation and how diseases like this, this whole business, how people constantly try to make sense of what's happening to them, how it works. It's an exploration of all those theories and the question of what you do with the Alzheimer's patient and how they should be treated. We were fortunate enough to be able to take care of my father in his home.

He always had a horror of being placed in a nursing home of some sort. He lived his life out at home until finally cancer of the prostate took him. We didn't do any of the things that you do for a person with cancer of the prostate to prevent it from killing him. We just let that take its course, and that took him out. He was going through this whole business in the late seventies.

*It certainly sounds like a very confessional approach. On that subject, do you think that Walker wove much of his personal life directly into his novels?*

That's very good that you ask that because I never knew anything about Walker's life until I read Jay Tolson's book. I knew about the Walker that I knew here, and I knew that he'd had tuberculosis, but I never knew that he'd spent that year in Germany until we took that trip to New Orleans.

*Did you know about his parents?*

No, not then. He never talked about that. But he knew my father very well. He was a witness to it all. He would come out and visit Dad. One of the things that Walker did in life was to pay attention to the sick and the suffering. He was right there along with the rest of us.

*Did he help you to understand what was going on with your father from a medical perspective?*

None of us knew, as a matter of fact. In those days you could not diagnose the fact of Alzheimer's in a living patient. You had to wait for a thin section of the brain tissue to be examined following death, which I had done, and we did in fact document that it was Alzheimer's and not something else. The reason for that was that I had some life plans to make of my own, and in those days we weren't sure how much of this was genetic. He'd had some things happen with his siblings that caused me to worry and wonder about it. We now know that there seems to be only a very small tendency on the part of descendants of Alzheimer's patients to suffer from the ailment themselves. It doesn't seem to me to be genetic particularly.

But Walker didn't know anything about it. In many ways, Walker was more naive medically than I was. The nature of my practice was such that I got called upon to get expert very quickly on all kinds of little byways of medicine, and I knew a lot more about some things in medicine than Walker did. He had left his medical lore very shortly after his internship. He continued to have an interest in it, particularly in mental illness, but he didn't know an awful lot about other things. He had the tools to find out about something.

*Have you ever recognized yourself in Walker's fiction?*

There is a passing reference to the kind of thing that Walker and I would have talked about in *Lancelot*, where he talks about the cajolery that goes on in getting one of your servants out of a jam. The main character goes to a friend of his who's a racist and says, "Now look, this is my nigger, and you've got to leave him alone, he's a nice fella." That sounds like some of what we encountered. But I don't think I see myself in any of Walker's work, certainly not as a character. I'd be very surprised if anything like me showed up. Walker wasn't the sort of writer who did that. I do it. But I don't think Walker ever did that consciously. There is a suggestion that the aunt in *The Moviegoer* is an analogue for Uncle Will. I wouldn't have said anything like that to Walker. As a matter of fact, something happened to him one day where somebody came to Walker's house and suggested that Uncle Will was gay, and Walker threw him out of his house. I think it was pretty generally known that he was, but Walker had a real problem with that.

*A problem discussing it or a problem with the fact of it?*

Well, there was a streak of homophobia in Walker. He never cottoned to the American Psychiatric Association's notion that homosexuals are not sick. He believed that it was a sickness. I think the reason that he thought that and clung so heavily to that view is that it was easier for him to think of gay people as being sick than to think of them as being perverse at heart, wicked and evil and damned, like the church said. I never knew Uncle Will and only read Uncle Will's poetry much later during my relationship with Walker. There's nothing in the poetry that would tip anybody off to that, I think. I suppose if you were looking for it, you could find it, but I was never that aware of it. He did, apparently, have a relationship with one of the blacks who worked for him for many years.

*Did you read Barry's "Rising Tide"? Did you think that he made too much of Uncle Will's homosexuality in that book?*

Yes, I did read it. It's an invaluable book, a very fine book. Apparently Uncle Will was a very interesting man and very near a saint from everything that I heard about him. I just can't comment about everything that's said about the Percy family in that book. Walker went from the old Stoic tradition to being right up there manning the barricades in the space of about fifteen years himself. I'm sure that Walker did things later in his life that Uncle Will would have been aghast at, but that's the way that life goes these days. Things are moving very fast.

*Would you comment some more on how Walker was helping your father and your family out during your father's last days?*

Well, in those days when I first knew Walker, my relationship to him was where he would come to parties at my parents' house and we would wind up doing all the talking, off in a corner somewhere, while everybody else was drinking and having a good time. In those days—I should say that Covington moves through phases in its socializing. There were years where they did treasure hunts, for example, and there were years where we had badminton parties at people's houses. Now Walker was not much of an athlete, but he came to all those parties. He and my mother and father were quite close, and he liked to discuss spiritual and philosophical matters with my mother, not so much with my dad. My father was a sort of good host who made all those things happen. With Dad, he was simply a good drinking buddy. But whenever a friend of his fell into any kind of misfortune like that, he would do anything he could to help either them or their family, the caretakers who were the satellites around them, as my mother and I were then.

*Would you talk more about the Great Books Club?*

We started off doing the Great Books program. Then after a while, we ran out of Great Books that they put out. We also got a little pissed off at them. I remember one particular thing was that they put in one of those books, *The Confidence Man: His Masquerade*, by Herman Melville. We all felt royally snookered. We all utterly hated that piece, to a man. We hated it so badly that I was delegated to writing a letter to the editors complaining. I recently sent copies of the letter that we all signed, including Walker, to Henry Mills for the Percy website. Our position was that we've all heard of bastards born of kings, and this was one of them.

It was a very lively group of minds. James Boulware was a member, Ed and Lucy Ballard, we had some in-resident conservatives, Bunt came, and notable for not coming was my wife Millie. She never came except one time. I never could figure out why Millie wouldn't do this because lit crit was her field. She was one of the most widely regarded lit crit people of theatrical literature in America and had recently left a position as chair of the Department of Theater and Speech at Chapel Hill. She came on the night that we did *Mother Courage* because she taught that play. All of us wanted Millie's insights into it, and she was good, really good. She brought stuff about Bertolt Brecht that none of us had access to.

There were a few other people—an Episcopal minister who came for a time, many others. They were just wonderful, lively evenings. I wish that we had recorded them. I did record one, which I sent to Lucy Ballard when she was recovering from a chemotherapy treatment. I sent it off to Lucy, and I guess it got lost among her personal effects. I'm sure it's lost forever. We would meet from around 8:00 to around 10:30, sometimes longer than that. After we got off the Great Books series, we would read the Best Short Stories collections that are put out annually. We're now reading the one that was guest-edited by Garrison Keillor. We've done the Best Essays, and we're doing the Best Spiritual Writing. We've also read through the canon of somebody's work. We did Raymond Carver, Ellen Gilchrist's books. Walker really didn't like Gilchrist very much. He was a very insightful critic, a wonderful critic. He could just pierce to the center of things. One year he was called upon to act as a judge in a contest, and we all read all of the stuff, and all of us picked the winner. It was a fiction contest. Walker asked us to participate with him to check himself and measure his opinions against ours. It was amazing how close all of us were in our evaluations of the work.

*Was there a certain angle he always took in your group, a certain style he was known for?*

I would say that Walker's style in the book meetings was that of a lurker. It would be mainly James and me being very terrierish and yapping after the fox, and Walker would sort of sneak in toward the end, after the major strings had been exposed and shouted about, and then he'd offer something extremely insightful. Our discussions didn't follow the rules. We would talk about movies that we'd seen, things on television. You know, Walker had extremely eclectic taste in popular culture. He was very big on *The Incredible Hulk*

TV show. He and Eudora Welty got into a chat about that once; they were both *Hulk* followers. I was a big *Star Trek* follower, like my father. I think it figured into our personal mythos about ourselves. It was interesting that Walker had the affinity for the Hulk—you know, the guy who would say, "You don't want to make me mad," and then he would turn into this monster of righteousness.

He had other little things like that too. You know, he was asked, along with a lot of other writers, what his favorite restaurant was, and he said he was fond of the Waffle House. He was always able to undercut pretension.

*Has the library or any other institution in Covington planned to do something to remember Walker?*

Well, the library is a rather sore point. After Walker's death, they wanted to name the library after him, and Louis Wagner, our old friend with the Confederate flag, botched that up and almost caused Walker's brother Phin to sort of call him out and have a duel with him. Cooler heads prevailed, though.

*The library in Greenville is named after Uncle Will.*

That doesn't surprise me. Well, Louis just died, and perhaps after Mrs. Wagner goes down the gray road, we may revive the motion to do it. Of course, the library does sponsor the Percy symposium, and that's very nice. It is true, though, that Walker never had much truck with the library. If he wanted to read a book, he just bought it or borrowed it from somebody. He was not a great patron of the library.

*What went on with the move to name it after him?*

I wasn't directly involved in it, but I know that Louis was up in arms about it. The mention of the name "Walker Percy" in the presence of Louis Wagner was fightin' words. He really was a thorn in the side of the school board. They were really hacked at having that whole thing drug up. That was a battle they didn't want to have to fight. They were really unhappy. There was a really quick flurry of activity that happened in the week or two after Walker's death, and I was so distressed about other aspects of it that I wasn't directly involved in it.

*Can you recall, from the discovery of Walker's cancer, the events of his last days?*

I can't give you a terribly clear idea of what the end game was like.

What I have to tell you is sort of oblique. But when Walker was first diagnosed, we didn't think it was going to be all that serious. He always downplayed it and made very light of it. He was going through the process of writing a Jefferson Lecture at that time. Then suddenly he was making all those trips up to the Mayo Clinic. I don't remember when I learned of it, that something should have been picked up but just hadn't been done at the proper time, but it was obvious that he then became a very sick man. I went out and visited with Walker when it became pretty obvious that the chemotherapy was taking a toll on him and he was in a pretty considerable amount of pain because I wanted to let him know that if he needed marijuana, he should ask for it. That is the only thing that we know of that can control the nausea associated with the kind of therapy that he was getting.

Walker always had a very delicate nutritional balance. He ate like a bird. One of the problems in his life—this isn't very well known, but I think one of the biographers mentions it—was that he would develop constrictions of the esophagus, which made it difficult for him to get food down from time to time. One reason why he was so thin was because he did have these problems of simply taking food into his system. I knew that this was going to cause problems for him if he was having constant bouts of nausea, so I went out and told him that if he wanted to get marijuana, there was a way of doing it. It had been made legal in Louisiana, although that's by state law. There may have still been some sort of federal barrier to that. But there was one dispensary available that would dispense Marinol, and I told him that he should go for it. The conversation that we had—there were some other people around the house at that point, he was not yet bedridden, and there were some other people visiting—but we walked out on the front porch, and Walker said, "You know, the fellow that wrote that piece called 'Nausea,' I don't think that he really ever experienced it." And I told him what he should do about it. He never told me whether he actually did or not, but we all thought that he was going to make it at that time. Then when I heard that they had given him extreme unction, the roof caved in. It was just grief, all over the place, and then he became too sick to visit. I never saw him in his last hours. He had a black woman that was staying pretty much around the clock with him—I think it was Carrie [Cyprian]. I have heard that she was a great comfort to him during that time, and the hospice program was very helpful. It was fairly new at that time. It was started by several of us over at the Episcopal church, and I was glad then that we had started it, if only for Walker's sake.

*Other than the situation in the library, did the community recognize him at that point? Was there simply an obituary. Was anything else written about him?*

In the community, I remember being royally pissed off at the Roman Catholic church. The funeral was at the Abbey, and the archbishop didn't come, and I thought that was just tacky as hell. He was supposed to have come, but he didn't. He was confirming people in a confirmation class that day and couldn't spare the time. I just felt that that was really—if Patrick Samway could fly in from New York, the archbishop could have come across the causeway. But the church was filled to overflowing at the Abbey. It was quite an occasion. I can't recall anything as well attended, except for Midnight Mass.

So far as in the community, I don't remember. I can't connect with that. I guess I was so involved with my personal feelings that I wasn't paying attention.

*What do you miss most about him?*

I suppose one of the things I miss most is that there are areas of interest that we never explored. For example, I never showed him any of my own writing, with the exception of a few poems that I gave him and which he returned with a very kind note. Now that I'm going to seriously be doing something like this myself, it would be lovely to have him around to do all those things that he did for so many other people. You know, of course, the story about *A Confederacy of Dunces*? I almost edited that book. He gave it to me to read. That little epic saga is a whole afternoon's story in itself. The manuscript that I was shown had some freaky things in it. It looked as if the typist might have gotten pages out of order or something, and there were areas that didn't really make much sense. I never actually read the published version of the book, having worked on it as I did, and subsequently it turned out that I wasn't needed as an editor. But Walker was always doing things like that for people. I miss that. That sounds incredibly crass, though. There are so many other things that I miss about him—his wonderful sense of humor, of course. It was irreplaceable, and it was really different, on an interpersonal level, than it is in the writing. He was a marvelous oral storyteller, and he would tell stories on himself. There was the time that he drove down to the post office with Sweet Thing, his little corgi, in the car, and he was getting back into his car and there was a black lady in the car next to him. He looked into his truck, and both windows were down, and he said, "Well hi, Sweet Thing, how are you gettin' on?" And the lady next to him said, "I'm doing fine, Sugar, how are you?" This was the kind of story that you would hear all the time.

# John "Red" Smith Jr., Tradesman & Raconteur
COVINGTON, LOUISIANA

*H. J. Smith & Sons Hardware was founded on 4 July 1876. It is the oldest hardware and general store in St. Tammany Parish, housing unique artifacts from the history of Covington, such as a dugout cypress canoe and a lead coffin. The store is located near the fork of the Bogue Falaya and Tchefuncte Rivers. Red Smith, grandson of H. J. Smith, now owns and operates the store with his sons. I have been told that if any one person has anything to say about Covington and the people who have shaped the community, it is Red Smith. This interview was conducted in the store one morning while Smith was looking over the mail. It was early in the morning, but the store was already in full swing, full of Smiths and customers. Smith met me at the counter and didn't hesitate to tell me about himself, when asked.*

I was born in New Orleans, December the 18th, 1919, and I started in this store when I was ten years old—it was my grandfather's store. At that time, my grandfather had what was like a cotton exchange. He would finance seeds, feeds, and fertilizer to a farmer, and they would grow a cotton crop and they'd bring the cotton crop down here and store it in his warehouse until the commodity prices got right in New Orleans. Then they'd ship it on a schooner over to New Orleans. Grandfather's old store is now a museum. That was the original store—the cotton scales, the cotton products, and the pictures of how they harvested and baled the cotton and all that.

He built that store on Columbia Street. People used to come down here to bring their cotton and they'd trade. He built on Columbia Street because two blocks from his store was the point of embarkation for the river that took the schooners to Lake Pontchartrain where they'd cross. They'd come up to this landing right here by his store, load and unload their produce and cotton. Of course, there was a lot more stuff than cotton. There was timber, there was bricks, there was food, there was all sorts of things that were available that were produced in this part of the country. Back in those days, a lot of wild game was shipped into New Orleans.

New Orleans has always had fine restaurants, so they'd get the ducks, the deer, the rabbits, and the squirrels and send them to New Orleans. There was no laws about harvesting that stuff. The people had sense enough not to completely deplete the supply, you didn't really need these restrictive laws on taking game.

Things were close. A lot of people couldn't afford much. People would come in here, the farmers would come in and run an account, and my grandpa used to always ask them, "What do you have for collateral?" Well, a guy might have two cows, or he might have a corn crop coming in or a cotton crop coming in. Occasionally, when the cotton crop failed—like on account of the boll weevil—it would be real close.

[A customer walks up with a string trimmer and says, "Feel that. See the corners on it? You can edge a sidewalk with that," and moves on.]

So that's the way it was. Of course, it's been modernized, and we've paved the streets, and got sewer and water and all the commodities in here. Before, there was what they called the ox lots. Guy by the name of John Wharton Collins came from England, and he's the one that dedicated Covington—he didn't dedicate it by the name of Covington, but it eventually became named Covington. He had in the middle of each square a small square, so as the lots backed up to that square, people had their outhouses, chicken houses, bird pens, dog pens, animal pens, horses or mules, whatever. They had access to the ox lots as usable property, but they didn't own it. It was public property.

*I noticed that no stores had built on the center of each block, that it was all used for parking.*

We tried—my grandfather had a cotton warehouse and blacksmith's shop back there, and they made him move it. The ox lot was dedicated to the purchasers of lots around the square. "The purchasers of lots would have the use, and the privilege, and the control of the streets, alleyways, and waterways, and timber trees"—that's on a dedication hung up there in my office. We got in a big lawsuit and the city threw us off, said we couldn't use public property. But we said the land is dedicated to the use of public property *by the surrounding property owners.* We got into a twenty-year lawsuit over that.

*It's interesting to see all the growth on Highway 190 outside town. That area outside town and this part of Covington seem like two different places.*

Well, it is, that's why people are trying to get into Covington. They're trying to get away from the speedy living, what they call anxiety, stressful living, everybody trying to run across the street before the other guy gets there. We've got to the point that we still have a terrific increase, but it's nothing like you saw on 190. And the other highways—25, 21—got people coming in here bumper to bumper. I've got some customers who live in Tylertown, 27 or 28 miles from here, and those people commute to New Orleans, which is another 50 miles, so this man's commuting to New Orleans, going about 80 miles, maybe more, depending where he's going. I say to them, "How can you tolerate that?" One guy said to me, "I've got an apartment in New Orleans. We don't have that much continuous work in New Orleans, but when we do, we'll stay over there for maybe two or three nights and go back home." In my day, you used a horse and buggy to get around here, until about 1912, when my dad came up with one of the first automobiles around here.

*Related to the town and Walker Percy being here, at what point did people in the town even know what he did for a living?*

He was kind of a recluse. He never associated too much with my type of person because I ain't an intellectual. He was, and he'd associate with the Friends of the Library, people of that nature, but I can't tell you much else about what he did. I didn't know that he made a living writing books, supposedly he was a doctor. I don't know whether he got lung trouble or some problem that he had, but he had to get away from it, and I think he came over here then to Covington. The only thing I know about him is that he called Covington a "non-place." I wasn't quite sure why he stayed here because a non-place, in my definition, would be an undesirable place. So why'd he come over here to a non-place to live? I haven't figured out why he did that or who I can talk to to figure that out, now that he's dead. Evidently, he didn't make too much of a swath around here because he don't have anything in his name—not a street, or a library, or a bookstore, or anything else. But he was a nice guy. I liked him. I talked to him occasionally when he'd come in here, but I never got really involved in asking him what he did or what his motives for being over here were. He bought some birds from here and wanted some wild birds. I had one that he needed, and I gave it to him. You're not supposed to sell the wild ones. It was a wood duck. He had a little pond behind his house. I think he had somebody clip their wings so they wouldn't fly. That was the biggest association I had with him, over that bird. I never did go down there and see it. He invited me down there several times to visit him, but I didn't go. I was always busy. Hell, I was in the process of raising a family and running this business. We had seven children.

[Aside, to a regular customer: "How you doin'?"

"Okay, how you doin'?"

"All right, thank you."

"Good to see you."

"Good to be seen too, I'll tell you."

"You're right. When you get up in age, it's just good if you're around."

"With all the aches and pains and problems, yeah."

"Well, you know I'm fortunate in that I have arthritis, and it don't hurt. I'm stiff in the joints and all, and once in a while a little achey, but nothing to complain about, you know."

"Well, I know the feeling because I was stiff in the joints once, and by the time they got me home, my wife was beatin' me in the back with a baseball bat and said to stay out of those joints."

"She had to loosen you up, did she?"]

*Have you taught your boys how to properly tell stories and keep up with the customers so it won't be so quiet during the times when you're at home?*

I tell you, we got that museum, and the schools will bring their children to see it. For a while I was so aggravated and busy that I couldn't go in there and do it. You gotta go in there with a clear mind because these kids, they'll ask you some questions that will really embarrass you. I used to let my sons go do that. I went over in there one day to listen to my boy, I was standing in the doorway there where he couldn't see me. These kids were waiting there, and he asked them, "Do you know how tough it was when I was a kid? Do you realize, would you believe, that we had a television with no remote? We had to get up, and go over there, and punch that button." And the kids, they all sat there with their eyes open, their mouths open. He said, "And another thing I'll tell you about how tough it was. We had an automobile with no air-conditioning. Can you imagine anything as primitive as that?"

*You ought to be proud that you have your family established in the business like this.*

That's the reason I'm in here. I'm eighty years old. I ought to be at home digging in the garden or something or sitting there watching television. I was in the hospital with six bypasses and a stroke for six weeks, and when I got back up here, I learned to keep my mouth shut. They were doing a better job than I was. They can handle it. One boy started here when he was eleven, and the older brother, he started here early, and when he was twelve, he was doing the work of an adult. Not physically, because he wasn't that strong, he was still little, but mentally. He was ordering stuff, stocking stuff, marking up stuff, billing stuff. My wife helped him a lot, she ran the books. My boys, they started early. I look around today, and these kids are out walking the streets, in trouble constantly. We're raising a bunch of gangsters. But I'm glad to have my family here. It's like a family reunion every day. Momma's gone, though. Momma left me in November of 1994. That wasn't supposed to be. I was supposed to go first because I was ten years older than she was.

*I recall the article you mentioned, where Dr. Percy referred to Covington as a "non-place." I think that maybe he liked it. I'd just as soon move here as anywhere I've been myself.*

Maybe that's what it was. Maybe a non-place meant no rushing, no fighting, no discrimination, you can't tell. I don't know. I tell you what, though, they got some people coming over from New Orleans now, and they're bringing New Orleans over here. I heard a coach tell me, he said, "The people come over here from New Orleans," said, "they bring their kids over here, and they want to tell us how to run the damned ball teams." He said, "I resent it." I said well you can't resent it because two reasons. Number 1, they got more votes than we got. All they got to do is go appeal to the government, and that's all the politicians hear, how many votes, and then of course how much money you got, that's what they do. But they come over here, and they say, "This is the way we did it in New Orleans." Well, why in the hell did they leave New Orleans? But another reason, I told him, is that with all them New Orleans people coming in here, we've got the finest damned doctors in the state of Louisiana here in Covington. In my time, there was two doctors, horse and buggy doctors. One of them didn't even have an office. You'd get in touch with him and he'd go to your house. Had to go get him on horseback. You've got to consider that, you've got to consider that if you didn't have that, if you didn't have the New Orleans people to help us with our hospitals, to help us with our business. Well, four families are in my store now, four families trying to make a living. Well, it ain't no big fine living, but it's better than going across the lake, riding that causeway two times a day, not only the time, but the exposure you take to getting in a wreck. You got these eighteen-wheelers, man, they'll grind you up in a second. They got guys making three or four runs to New Orleans a day with 26 to 28 yards of gravel. They don't see anything. They're full of narcotics, them boys. Not all of them, but some of them. They don't even see another car coming.

*In one of his earlier books, Dr. Percy writes about some characters who are civil rights workers from up North coming into the South. How was Covington involved with civil rights struggles?*

Percy, I think, was involved in that, he and Nikki. Nikki Barringer was an attorney. Walker Percy was a doctor who wasn't practicing and was writing books. So as far as him getting into the community, well, I don't know. There were a few people, agitators, who came in here. I think in the end, Nikki and Walker saw the light, and they gracefully backed off because the thing couldn't work the way those other people wanted it. We were lucky. The closest trouble we had was in Bogalusa. A man was sent up there to agitate. Some group trained him to infuriate and inflame people. They were going to storm the courthouse up there, and a tough cop, a state trooper, was sent up there to stop it.

# Carrie Cyprian, Housekeeper
COVINGTON, LOUISIANA

*Carrie Cyprian, an African American woman who worked for the
Percys as a housekeeper, lives just outside of Covington, down a small
country road near the woods. Her house is almost 200 years old, and
it is surrounded by large live oaks. She said that Walker Percy loved
her trees—that they "fascinated him." As we were talking about the
house, she told a story about how Percy tried to get shutters from the
old St. Peter's Church to help her fix the place up—"he was always
thinking about me and my family," she explained. After going inside,
the first thing Cyprian said was that her furniture was "piecemeal," as
if to apologize, but it looked wonderful. The house is filled with tables,
chairs, sofas, and clocks that she inherited from relatives, and pictures
of her family are everywhere. Virtually every item is associated with
a family memory. One of Cyprian's grandchildren alternated between
chasing a ball across the floor and banging with his toy hammer. We
sat in the parlor and watched the grandchild play while Cyprian began
talking about her time with the Percy family.*

I worked for the Percys. They were very good to me, and I came to know
them very well. I knew Dr. Percy as a person, not just as a celebrity.
I was born in Covington, grew up here, and moved away only for
a while when I got married. I came back here with my children in
1964, and Dr. and Mrs. Percy were the first family to give me a job.
I was looking for a job when I moved back, and a friend of mine,
Ina Mae Griffin, was working for them and she was getting ready
to leave. I went and started ironing first for them, and when Ina
Mae left, I just took the position that she had, cooking and taking
care of the house, ironing, and being with Anne and Mary Pratt,
things like that. They were both very down-to-earth people, and I
did not know at that time that he was a celebrity. They were just
very nice people to work with. For a while I did not know that he
was trained to treat people medically. I knew that he was home,
writing a lot, and then I found out that he was a writer. He began
to ask me questions about ironing when I used to iron, how to use

the heat and the cold, how did I use starch, and stuff like that. He would ask me and Ina Mae stuff like that.

He really wanted to know about people. He liked people. He wasn't a person that had a lot of people in all the time—he had people, just not all the time. But he was particularly concerned about people, and how you live, you know, what made you tick. He was that type of person. And he was a very easy person to talk to. I'm saying "he," but the two of them, Dr. and Mrs. Percy, were like that. Coming here, I didn't have transportation, and he didn't mind getting up to come and get me and bring me back home, and of course I had to have special rules, and he didn't mind adjusting to those special rules. My kids were small and they were in school, and they would catch the bus home. I told the Percys that I liked to be here when the bus picked up my children in the morning, and I liked to be home when the bus dropped them off. When we bought this house, there weren't any neighbors, there was just space out here. And they didn't mind, they catered to that. I mean, they were concerned about my children and what we had, and how we were living, and whether I was able to make it, you know, and every once in a while they would give me extra money for my children to make sure my family was being taken care of. They were very concerned about the people they knew. I came to think about it, that it wasn't just me, it was about people, he wanted the people in Covington to do better. He wanted the people in Covington to live better. I think he was one of the first people that started the credit union so that the people would have a credit union here where everybody would be able to do something. He would talk about how he wanted to help people, and this included black people, all people, no matter who they were. He wanted to help people, and she did too.

There were only two books that he wrote while I was there because he did a lot of articles. I think the names of those books were *The Moviegoer* and *Gentleman, Gentleman.*

*"The Last Gentleman?"*

Right. Those were the books he wrote. They had a little dog named Sweet Thing, and he liked to walk. Dr. Percy would walk just about every day, and he took his nap just about every day. The dog got lost around the post office area, and my husband, who worked at the post office, he found it. Dr. Percy was so grateful he gave him a book and autographed it. It was *Gentleman, Gentleman*. My husband is still very proud of that book. Dr. Percy was just a giving person, not just financially, but whatever he could do, he helped the community. He is very, very, very much missed.

*So Dr. Percy was involved with starting the credit union?*

I know he was part of it because he joined me into it when it first got started. I didn't know anything about it until he told me that he had signed me up and I could take my checks there and deposit what I wanted, whatever.

*Do you know of other involvement that he had with the community?*

Well, all the black movements that went on, he helped. He was trying to get black people into law enforcement and different positions that would help them. All the integration that went on in Covington that I know of, he was involved in them. He tried to put people into things that would benefit the black people and help the community as a whole, not pull it down, but help the community. These are the things that Mr. Percy did, and Mr. Percy's family was 100 percent behind him.

*Father Boulware, who used to be out at the Abbey, mentioned how Dr. Percy was interested in learning how people did things, like you talked about with ironing. Was he interested in how you cooked too?*

Oh, he loved my cooking. I remember one year when I was fixing a Thanksgiving dinner and I stuffed a turkey. I lost the little thing that you put in the turkey to hold the dressing in, and he went and got his surgical kit and he and I did surgical work on the turkey to close it. And he loved the way I cooked liver. I'd smother it with onions, and he loved the way that I kept it very tender, the way that he liked. My aunt and my mother both were cooks and nutritionists, so I learned that if you didn't use the right amount of heat on the liver, you would toughen it, and it would get hard and be difficult to eat. I learned that you have to cook liver on a hot fire, the skillet has to be very, very hot, and I always used margarine or butter in the skillet, and just barely added the flour, almost pass it under the flour, and you put it in the hot skillet and turn it right quick, turn it over both sides right quick. Then you take it out, and you put your onions and your seasoning in there, then you lay it back on there and turn the heat down and you steam it. There were many things that he loved. I introduced him to squash pie—he became fond of that, and he loved my pecan pies. Dr. Percy loved my biscuits too. He was a wonderful man to work for.

Another thing that I liked about Dr. Percy is that he was interested in my family, whether my family had food, whether my children had clothes. When I would get sick—I would get sick a lot, and still do, that's how I am—when I would get sick, sometimes I would have to stay home from work a week or so or better. My job was always there. And if I would get sick there, doing something, and would have to come home, they would bring me home and they would not cut my pay. Back in those days—I worked for Dr. Percy in the early sixties, and I must have worked for Dr. Percy until the eighties, and in the eighties I worked for Anne, their daughter, and took care of David, the first baby that she had. It wasn't like a job. It was like you were taking care of your family, and they made me feel that way. When someone would come, they would want to introduce me to them. They would never say, "This is my maid" or "This is the person who works for me." They would say, "This is Carrie, one of our friends." They made me feel like a friend. Even now, there are times when Mrs. Percy picks up the phone and just calls me to see how I am, and I call to see how she's doing. We just have a very, very special relationship.

*That's wonderful. Now when Dr. Percy was involved with the community and the civil rights work here, how did the rest of the town seem to react to that? Was there a lot of resentment in Covington, or did people accept things more easily?*

I think it was better than the average town. There was always some resistance, you know. I would know about the resistance that the black people would have, but as far as any resistance that the white people or the Cajun people would have, I didn't know about their part. I do know that Dr. Percy would go out of his way to help. I remember that once Dr. Percy wanted my husband to take a position at the post office, and he was one of the first blacks to take a position at the post office, and we got threats. I remember one day I was off from work and I was here alone and there were no neighbors here, just woods all around, and I got a threat. Someone called me and said that there was a bomb under the house, and I didn't know what to do. My instinct was to pick up the phone and call Dr. Percy, and I did. Before I knew anything, policemen were all out here, my protection was here. We were trying to figure out why this had happened to me. It was because of the fact that my husband was a politician too, and his name would come up in the paper occasionally.

*Did you ever read any of Dr. Percy's books?*

No, no, I haven't. I did start reading some papers once, a sketch of his life. Mrs. Percy brought me some clothes that I was gathering to give to the needy, and in those clothes were some loose papers, where someone had roughly drafted some of his life history. I took them out and I had them on the table at the place where we took those clothes, the Community Service Center, and during the time I wasn't working on anything, I would read some of it. I was trying to read some of that, but I think somebody took them and I never really got to read it.

*Could you talk to us more about the family, including the Percys'*
*daughters? How did you adjust to working with Anne and her*
*hearing problem?*

Well, when I got there, Anne was already born and Mary Pratt was a pretty good-aged girl. Anne did take a lot of devotion, but in that home, there was a lot of love. I love, and I know about love. I came up in a family of love. But I learned to share it from that family. They didn't care whether you returned that love, they just loved. Mary Pratt and Anne were two wonderful young people. Anne, even with her hearing and speaking problem, was treated as a normal child. This was amazing to me because I had been in places where there were children who had things wrong with them and they were treated totally different. Lots of children like that are pushed aside because their folks just can't understand what to do with them. But anyway, Anne was treated just like Mary Pratt, she was even talked to just like Mary Pratt. I have never signed to Anne. I have written notes occasionally for Anne. But I would talk to Anne like I'm talking to you, and I would make sure that she stopped and looked at me as I spoke, and I would speak slowly, but Anne understood whatever I said when I talked to her. I had a problem at first understanding her because she didn't like to write notes, she just wanted to talk. She would get excited, and sometimes I couldn't understand, and sometimes I had to hold her and say, "I don't know what you're saying. Now speak to me, tell me." And then she would get real frustrated and go in her room and shut the door because she was angry at me. And she'd write little notes and put them on the door that said, "Do Not Disturb." I thought it was really cute.

But they were both treated the same. Anne had a lot of tutors coming in to help her, but Anne went to a regular school, just like the other children, and she was a good student. She made good grades. They went to the Catholic school. She was in a school where people spoke. Mrs. Percy lost a lot of time with her, and Dr. Percy, and Mary Pratt would lose time with her, and I lost a whole lot of time. A lot of times there were things I should have been doing in the house and if Anne was home, I would lose time with Anne because I just loved being with her. That's why, when she was married and needed somebody with her little son, I was there. I just love being with her. I realized that he wasn't hearing either, her first child, while I was with him. It was a while before his problem was detected because he was a lot like Anne, active and always doing things. But it was little things that made me notice. When I would get behind him and say things, he wouldn't respond, and I told Mrs. Percy that I didn't think he was hearing well. I got sick then and started having to have back surgery from an accident years before, so I couldn't keep up with him as well as I would have liked to.

*What was Mary Pratt like?*

When she was younger, Mary Pratt was very social, she was interested in doing a lot of things. She liked boating, you know the river was right behind their house. She was very lively and full of life.

*Which parents did they take after?*

I don't think that either of them was much like him because of the quietness that he carried. He portrayed a very quiet, isolated way—he wasn't isolated, but he portrayed that. You know, just to look at him and see him go into his room where he would write, that isolated him a lot. But he would come out for his meals, come out for his walk, come out to be with the children, come out to be with the dog. He would come out to spend time with the family. But Mrs. Percy was there, open, all the time for the children, for whatever they needed. As far as the programs they were in at school and things like that, he would be there for that, but his writing took a lot of time. He wasn't just out there with the children in the living room, in the den, or out in the yard like Mrs. Percy was. Both the children were outgoing children. Anne would like to go in the boat, she would like to do things in the yard, she would like to go with friends, like Mary Pratt would. But Dr. Percy never portrayed that outgoing way.

*It's been said that he was very disciplined with his writing.*

Yes, he was. But his family was important to him, so it was easy for him to set aside certain times for his family. But he had certain hours that he spent just writing. He would go into his room and he would just write, and he wouldn't come out until maybe twelve o'clock or twelve-thirty to eat, and I'd have the food on the table for him. After he would eat, sometimes he would take a walk, and he would take a nap, and then he would go back. He really kept office hours as near as possible there, in the house with his wife.

*How did he react to distractions like people showing up or calling during his writing time?*

There were times that he took phone calls, but Mrs. Percy would take a lot of them. If there was something that he was really trying to put together and Mrs. Percy was gone, he would tell me that he wasn't taking phone calls and I would just take a message. As I say, he was a people person, but not—he loved people, but he wasn't out there in the crowd all the time.

His concern was that betterment, what he could do to make life better, what he could do to make life better for the world that he existed in, and people were in his world, so he was concerned with them. You've seen his pictures haven't you?

*Yes, ma'am.*

Well, when you look at his pictures, what do you think? This is a man totally isolated, that would isolate himself. But inside he wasn't, he wasn't that way.

*His pictures show him with that sort of smile that suggests he was amused at something.*

He kept that smile all the time. All the time he had that smile. Everything was just amazing to him. And you would think with the mind he had—he had the most brilliant mind I ever recognized in a person—you would think that he wouldn't be amused about little things. But everything amused him. I remember John Walker, the oldest grandson, he wanted to go walking with him, and you know how children are, they never want to stop. Dr. Percy wanted to do something else, so he told John Walker that he couldn't go walking because he had a bone in his leg. And the child fell for that, and Dr. Percy was so amused by that, he was so amazed. He enjoyed his family like that. He was a wonderful man. Covington was blessed to have him.

*Did he ever talk to you about why he came to Covington, why he liked it here?*

No, he never talked to me about why he came to Covington, but after I found out that he was a celebrity, or sometimes when he would be bringing me home, he would be so amazed about the countryside. A lot of this that's on Highway 36 was not there way back, thirty years ago. When the leaves would be on the trees, or when it would be changing, the leaves would be changing, like this time of year, that amazed him. I would say sometimes, I would ask him why he was so amazed at this. He would say that he liked the quietness of Covington. He liked the comfort that he has here. Sometimes it would rain, and I would be there and the rain would just come down, and I'd stand at the window and I'd watch the rain. Afterward, he would come out, and I would say, "Shhhh, smell the rain." I love that smell of the earth after it rains. And he would say he liked it too. He asked me about things, it looked like he was interested in my heritage, where I came from. I would tell him about my grandmother. She was a midwife, and she treated people with certain herbal teas, being Indian, and I would tell him about the pine needles that we would rub our iron on to make the clothes iron smoothly and certain bushes that I could go out into the woods and pick and make tea and what it would be good for. I don't think he was really learning anything from me, he was just acting interested. The man was too wise to learn anything from me.

Now Mrs. Percy, while he was writing, would be involved with the children, take care of the house, or plan some entertainment for people who would be coming in, or arranging certain meetings that he would have. There were a lot of people coming to him just for him to look at their writing, to see if it was worth being published. Her life was full of things like that. I remember after Dr. King was assassinated, my sister wrote a poem. She was always writing poems, and she wanted me to take a poem about that for him to look at. And I carried that poem with me to work for about two weeks because I didn't know how to ask him. So many people would come, and he would be so busy, I just didn't know how to ask him. So one day he was sitting at the table, and I took out the poem and I showed it to him. And he showed that there were some things that she needed to do to it, but he liked it.

He was a man that never really would say how he felt about too many things. It was shown in what he did. It was like when I didn't even know that he was a part of this credit union until he had signed me in. But he was working in it. And a lot of the meetings, the civil rights meetings that he would go to, I wouldn't even know that he was going until my husband would come back and he would talk about Dr. Percy being there. It was just a part of life to him. It was nothing big or something that he would brag about, it was just a way of living. He took that responsibility, and he felt like he had to shoulder it, and he just went on with it, just like taking care of his family, writing his articles, or whatever.

*Is there anything else that you think I should know about Dr. Percy?*

All I can say is that he was an extraordinary man in a very small town that hardly knew anything about him. He lived a life just as common as the people in Covington. They were right there with the people. I worked for other people, but with the Percys, it didn't feel like a job. It felt like I was helping friends, and I'm getting taken care of because I'm taking care of them, and that's the way it works. In most cities they have some kind of monument or something to say that this person was here or this person was there, but they have none of that for Dr. Percy. When you look back on all the things that he did for all the people here, it seems like something should be here to recognize that this is where Walker Percy lived, this is where he was, this is where his family still is.

*What kind of monument would be fitting for him?*

Because of the way I know him, I'd say a library or something like that. I wouldn't say a statue of him because that would be too open, too public, and he wasn't that type of person. Books and education would be more for him. A school or a library—something that represents him and his heartfelt desires. But not a statue. That's not him. He was a public man, but he wasn't *in* the public. His concern was for the public.

# Leroy Frick, Fellow Citizen
COVINGTON, LOUISIANA

*Leroy Frick and his wife, Helen (now deceased), came to know Walker Percy shortly after Percy's arrival in Covington. Frick, a former shipbuilder, recalled his friendship with Percy during my visit to the Frick home in Covington.*

When I first met Dr. Percy, he was an M.D. who had come to Covington for his health. He was interested in trying to help the colored people of the community. He and a couple of other doctors—Dr. Hill, Dr. Thompson—they all worked with a group of us, trying to get better jobs for the colored people. Instead of being janitors, they tried to help us get jobs as clerks, you know.

He was also interested in trying to get better housing for the black community. He sat here quite a few nights, and we were talking about trying to build homes, getting land where we could start a project to build them. It was a losing battle because they fought us every inch of the way. But he kept trying, and he came up with an idea for a credit union. We worked on that project and finally we got it started, and we had a little credit union over here on 31st Street. We finally got a little building built over there on Lawyer Barringer's land. He didn't charge us any rent. We had volunteers to build the building. It went on for about nineteen years, and then it joined to the credit union from Avondale in New Orleans, and they have a nice big building that's operating just like a bank now. It's called the Covington Credit Union now. Originally it was named after our group, the Community Council of Greater Covington, and we used our initials for the name.

He worked with us. He didn't work at the credit union after it was on its way, but he was always interested. He got Lawyer Barringer to let us build on his land, and every year, I think it was the first week after Easter, he would give Lawyer Barringer a rose. That was our rent, believe it or not, for the year. Religiously, Dr. Percy would go and buy this rose and go and present it to Lawyer Barringer. *Is this Nikki Barringer's family?*

Yes, Nikki Barringer helped us a great deal. This went on until Dr. Percy died. Before Avondale took over the credit union, Mrs. Emily Diamond was running the credit union. I think she ran it for the whole nineteen years. She was doing all that work for free. In the last year or two that she ran it, he [Percy] came up with the plan to pay her a hundred dollars a month, and he paid that salary. He was a very generous person. He was interested in the community where he lived, you know.

He also worked to try to get better jobs for the colored people. They would have meetings right here, the Council of Greater Covington. We worked to try to get land to build homes. We tried to get land so many times, but there was always some stumbling block, something to block us. But he worked on trying to help the colored people in Covington. I guess he figured the white people in Covington didn't need any help—they were doing alright on their own!

But like I say, he wasn't a well person. He came here for his health, but he worked to help us. He was liked by the people that knew him—there weren't too many people, I'd say, that knew Dr. Percy—but he was liked by the people that knew him.

*Was he a very private person?*

Well, being a writer, you know, it took up a good bit of his time. He had a store for his daughter, a bookstore, called the Kumquat. That was a project for his daughter, and he would go down there sometimes and sit up in his loft and work on his book—several books.

*Have you ever read any of his books?*

I read part of one, it was about Louisiana. I don't remember the name of the book. But like I said, he was a person who stayed pretty much to himself when he wasn't out trying to help other people.

He had this little group of doctors who were interested in doing what they could for the community. Dr. Charles Hill, Dr. Thompson—I don't remember his first name—and Dr. Malcolm Burns. It seems like there was another doctor, but it was long ago.

*Would you tell me about your background, your life leading up to the time you met Dr. Percy?*

Well, I was born in Covington. At different times I've lived in Baton Rouge, I've lived in Slidell, I've lived in Abita Springs, but Covington is my home. I've been in this home since 1958. I got to know Dr. Percy through the community group I told you about.

*Had you done any work for the community prior to getting involved with the Greater Covington group?*

The only thing I did before that was that I worked with a group from the Covington Athletic League for the kids who played baseball. My wife and I were always active—my wife was a teacher for twenty-five years in the parish. She taught in Covington schools and Abita Springs. We'd been active in trying to help get things going around here and trying to help the colored people, but Dr. Percy and Malcolm Burns and the others organized this little group. We would meet here. But as for how Dr. Percy was involved, we had another organization called the Bridge, and it was also something to help the colored people in the area to get better homes, plus give the kids something to do. It was named the Bridge because of bridging the gap between white and colored. That went on for quite a while. What grew out of that was the credit union. We tried to get jobs at the bank as tellers, as clerks at the supermarkets. Luckily we were successful in placing some in these positions. It didn't come fast, but eventually it came.

*You mentioned earlier the stumbling blocks you encountered in trying to buy land for housing in the area. What sort of obstacles did you encounter?*

It was opposition from the white people. They'd come in and block the projects. One project we tried to get was found out about, and the white people got with the parish and they just turned the project down. We were going to buy the land, and they got to the people who owned it, and they just told us no, they decided not to sell the land.

All the people involved in our little organization were very much hurt by this. It just seemed like you'd hit a brick wall. We had people who didn't even live on the road where this land was, they lived somewhere else, and they just came down and met with the city and the parish to block it. We had made arrangements on one project already with Abita Springs to get water, electricity, and to just have a nice subdivision, with light poles and underground wires, and it never materialized. They fought us toe and nail, I tell you.

Eventually, they got something around here, but not like that. There were two housing units that they built. One was around Florida Street and Columbia Street, out by the fairgrounds, and then in another part of Covington for black senior citizens. They were built by the Housing Authority, out of New Orleans. My wife was president of the Housing Authority group over here, and they named one of the units Helen Frick Village. The other one is named Carrie Owens. She was a schoolteacher here for years. Everybody was tickled to death that they were able to finally do that, to build nice houses for colored folks.

We built our house in 1958, and we were the first colored people to have a brick home in Covington. We bought this land in '58. A colored lady had a house right behind here and she owned this. We were able to get her to sell us part of the land. They had a street, but it was grown up and they had the culverts taken up. It was only a block long then. The street itself was grass. I had to get the town to put the culverts back down, and then we built the house. There wasn't a credit union then. I had to get financing from a colored insurance company in New Orleans, Standard Insurance Company.

*Would you tell me what the housing conditions were like back then?*

*Why was it so important to work for better housing?*

You haven't traveled up in the New Covington area, the colored area? The housing was very poor, mostly shotgun houses. Had quite a few of them that were owned by whites and rented to the colored. One man who owned a store in town had land and built two blocks of shotgun houses on it, and I lived in the first one he built. It was right over on Florida Street. Shotgun houses were the type homes they built back then. The Negroes didn't make much money on the jobs they had, and they wanted low rent, you know. So this one man had a big yard behind his store where he had saws, and he'd cut up all the lumber for the houses down there, and just bring it onto the land and build a little house. It was cheap enough—four dollars a week. They had a little back porch and a half bath—half of the back porch was a little bathroom. They were so small that you couldn't hardly put a heater in that little bathroom. I talked to him and got him to build me an extra room on the back, and he went up on the rent to six dollars a week, but he built a big room on the back and enlarged that bathroom a little bit. They didn't even have gas piped to the houses. I had a neighbor who had all kind of tools, he had a job to fix all kinds of leaking pipes. Anyway, he came over, and I bought a hot water heater to put in the house and a sink to put in the kitchen, and we piped all of that.

*Was there any sort of plumbing in the house already?*

We only had water in the bathroom, but we didn't have anything in the kitchen before I did that work. You had to go outside, out the kitchen door, onto the porch, and into the bathroom to fill up a pot of water. I had to buy the hot water heater—he didn't furnish that. I remember my brother saying, "You buying a hot water heater to put in another man's house?" And I said, "Yeah, but you're missing the point. I'm enjoying that hot water heater. I have to shave and bathe, and I don't have to heat a pot of water on the stove and carry it to dump in the tub nine or ten times."

That bigger bathroom and that extra room on the back made it nice. We had two daughters, and we could then make a living room out of the front room. We lived in that place for eighteen years. Then we got this land and found somebody to finance the house. There was a colored contractor who built it, and he was familiar with the Standard Insurance Company and helped me work it out to finance it.

There wasn't a blacktop then—the street behind me wasn't paved, and the street in front of me wasn't paved. Then when they got ready to pave the street that ran along the front, Mr. Red Smith owned that whole lot across the street, most of the block. I was out in the yard one Sunday evening and he was out riding around with his kids, looking around. They had a project to pave the streets of Covington then. He saw me and walked over and said, "Leroy, they getting ready to pave this street, and I was checking my property in Covington to see whether or not I would go along with it because it costs. They charge for it. Now if you want them to pave it, they're going to charge you for it."

I said, "Well, look at that house, it cost me something to build that."

He said, "Well, if you want it, I won't knock it. I'll go along with it."

He owned that whole lot, see, and he had to pay for his to get them back here, and his was most of that whole block. That's how we got the streets paved out here.

*You said that your group tried to get better jobs for people. Would you tell me about some of the work you had to do to support your family?*

Well, I was working in New Orleans. I worked at a plant, the Higgins plant, and we were building airborne lifeboats. They were building them so you could put them in planes and haul them places. We built them out of plywood—Mr. Higgins had his own plywood mill. During World War II, he had a big plant downtown where they built the PT boats. They had a great big building—it was so big that if you were inside it, you didn't even know it was raining outside unless you saw a truck drive through that was wet.

I worked in the boat division, and we built those plywood boats. After we'd finish with it, they'd move the hull to another section where they'd sand it all down and putty the holes with the screws in it. After they'd sand the boats down, they put them in an oven-like thing for a while, then they'd paint them and ship them out on rail. I don't know where they went after that.

*When did you come back to Covington?*

I didn't move over there. I had to travel back and forth everyday.

*But they didn't have the causeway built across Lake Pontchartrain then, did they?*

No, there wasn't no causeway. You had to go around through Slidell, the long way. It took you about two hours to get there in the morning and two hours to get back at night. We rode in a truck that picked up people along the way.

*I guess the pay was enough to justify all the travel?*

It was a whole lot better than what you could make around here at that time. They weren't paying much, but a dollar an hour was big money for us in those days.

*What could you have done in Covington?*

There wasn't much. You could have been a carpenter or a bricklayer— my brother was a bricklayer. I had worked at a boat builder here in Covington and learned how to paint boats, then went from there to Higgins. Later I left Higgins and went to a shipyard in Slidell, where they were building some boats out of plywood and oak. They called them net-tenders, and they were big boats, about 200 feet long. The bulkheads were double bulkheads of fir and oak. They had slabs of oak you couldn't pick up—they had to use cranes to pick those slabs up. They'd go out there and mark water lines on that wood and what the cut was supposed to be, and then they had a crane, and I worked with a band saw, cutting out all the frames.

*You still have all your fingers.*

Yeah! The only hurt I got was when that big old band saw got me while I was cleaning out all the sawdust from under it. I stuck one tooth under my fingernail a little bit. They would break, those band saws. Right before a blade would break, you could hear it go "tick, tick, tick." When I'd hear that "tick, tick," I'd hit a red button and get out of the way. It didn't have much space, but that blade could fly loose and kill you. Somebody was always telling you tales about somebody getting killed, cut in half by a band saw. I kept one eye on what I was cutting and one eye on that red button. Before I got to the band saws, I was working on a crew to plank the boats, but the superintendent got me off of there to work with a four-man crew on a brand-new saw. They had two men on each side of my saw, and they had this crane there, and when the planks would go through my saw, they'd load the wood on a dolly and the crane would take it off. We cut out all the lumber for six big net-tenders.

*Were you always in the boat-building business?*

More or less, until I went to Sears. The group never had to help me, thank God. We were trying to help others. My wife taught school and I worked. I worked with the boats for seventeen years. They didn't have benefits—no insurance, no retirement. It took that long for me to get a job that had some kind of retirement benefits.

But I'd had worse times on jobs. Back when I was young, I used to work for the Chevrolet dealer, and he'd send me off to take cars different places, to dealers. I had to go into Mississippi for them every week, between Laurel and Hattiesburg. First week I worked for them, I had to bring an old truck back and my brother was with me. I can't remember exactly where it was, but I pulled into a service station and the guy came out, stopped about twelve feet from the car, and said, "What you want?" I told him I wanted some gas, and he said, "We don't wait on niggers." I looked at my brother and he said to get on out of there, so I pulled on out and made it to another town. I wasn't out of gas yet, but I barely had enough to get to the next town. "We don't wait on niggers." I started to stop at another one, but when I got down the road, there was a big old sign, about 4 x 8. You'll never guess what they had on that sign: "Nigger, read and run. If you can't read, run anyhow." That was back in '38.

*How did Covington handle the changes with civil rights?*

This was one of the better places. Covington was better than Hammond during those days or Slidell. One black man did something in Slidell, and they drug him through the streets. They hung one here, down by the courthouse on the big oaks, but that was before my time. But Hammond was the same as Slidell. You'd go to the train station in Hammond, and they had separate places for you to go, but you couldn't stand out in front of the depot until the train came in—they didn't allow colored people out in front of the train station. You had to stay in a room until the train came. Whatever train you were catching, when it came, you could come out, but you still had to walk about half a block to get on the part of the train where colored people rode. There were some places you'd go through on the train in Mississippi where they'd pull the shades down on the windows where the colored people were. You'd stop, and they'd holler stuff at you, "Nigger this" and "Nigger that." It's strange how life was then. But this little town, like I say, was better than Hammond or Slidell in those days. Those towns were pretty rough. They were hard on you.

*Was there resistance to establishing the credit union?*

No. Mr. Barringer, Nikki, let us build, and they couldn't stop that. After we had the credit union, we had our meetings over there.

*Did you know Dr. Percy well outside the Greater Covington group?*

I did. Dr. Percy and my wife christened Dr. Malcolm Burns's son over in Madisonville. He had a white godfather and a black godmother, and his daddy named him John Martin, after Dr. Martin Luther King and the president. John Martin. When that same kid made his first communion, Dr. Percy and Mrs. Percy came by and picked us up and took my wife and I with them to the other side of Baton Rouge. We went by Malcolm's house and ate, and Dr. Percy and his wife picked us up. He was very nice, he and Mrs. Percy.

I work at the furniture store now, two days a week. We get old books that come through there from the library. I found this one book not long ago called *Dinner at the Mansion*, and I was thumbing through this book, and up jumped Dr. Percy's picture. He was at the Mississippi governor's house, the mansion, and they'd invited him for dinner and taken his picture. I thought that was nice. I started to bring the book home, but I didn't. If my wife was still living, I would've had to bring it home. She was very fond of Dr. Percy. We were married fifty-nine years, and she passed in 1996. Fifty-nine years—that's quite a stay.

My wife was an outgoing person. All the plaques and awards on our walls are hers—from the archbishop, the senior citizens program, the Catholic charities group, the child development center. That was her pet project, that center, the Regina Coeli Center. People used to say it "coaly," but it's "chelly." There's a proclamation from the mayor on her seventieth birthday. They called it Helen Frick Day, gave her a key to the city. It was on her birthday and we had a big party for her, and people gave gifts for the Regina Coeli Center.

*I see a picture of her and the Head Start program. Did she and Dr. Percy work together on that too?*

Yes. Anything good that went on in Covington during those times had the same group of people working for it. Anything good that went on here, my wife was in it. And Dr. Percy was in a lot of it too. Look at that wall behind you.

[Two walls in the home are completely filled with award letters and plaques recognizing Helen Frick's years of service.]

*I see: vice president of the League of Women Voters, vice president of Habitat for Humanity, St. Tammany Retired Teachers Association, the zoning commission for Covington, the zoning commission for St. Tammany Parish, Covington Historical Commission, the Council on Aging, St. Peter's Catholic Church Council, Covington Housing Authority. It says here that "the first public housing development in the City of Covington bears her name: The Helen Frick Village." Woman of the Year by the Covington Chamber of Commerce. That's really something. Did you have any idea when you married her what kind of lady you had gotten hold of?*

Well, I knew she was alright, but I didn't know all this would come to pass. She was so involved with things, it was natural that we'd come to know Dr. Percy. I feel very proud to have known Dr. Percy because of the type person he was. He was always willing to help somebody. He and my wife were the hub of so many good things in the community. This group, these people were willing to help.

# Sister Jeanne D'Arc, Teacher

## ST. JOSEPH ABBEY, LOUISIANA

*Sister Jeanne D'Arc joined the sisters of the order known as St. Scholastica in Covington after being educated in the order's school and has served the church as a teacher in parochial schools ever since. She shared her memories of Walker Percy from an office at St. Joseph Seminary College.*

*Arriving at St. Joseph Abbey for the first time was a special event for me. Walker Percy's funeral services were held here, and he was buried in the Abbey's cemetery, very near Sister Jeanne D'Arc's office, in recognition of his status as an oblate of the church. The Abbey is like this region of Louisiana in one respect—it has a U.S. zip code, but it is not "regular" America. It is impossible to walk to the seminary offices and not be struck by the unique visual blend of the Benedictine monastery, pine trees, azaleas, and Abbey church. It is always quiet at the Abbey, the kind of place where a person realizes that it is not only quiet enough to think but also so quiet that one absolutely must think. It was a bit surprising when Sister Jeanne D'Arc broke the silence to speak.*

I came to Covington to teach at St. Scholastica's. I'm originally from New Orleans. I've been in Covington most of the years since, other than some years in South America teaching and some studying in the Midwest. They closed the boarding school at St. Scholastica in 1974. There used to be many boarding students, but as time went on, we were getting more local students and it was getting to be more difficult to meet the needs of boarders and their expectations, so we've kept only the day school since 1974. It's been a girls' high school, from eighth grade on, for twenty-five years, and they are nearing 600 students now. In the days when I first came to St. Scholastica, that would've seemed a monumental number. Covington was still very much a small, summertime town when I first came, so you didn't have a lot of students from the area, but there were always some. Through the years, that number has grown, of course, and now the graduates are all local people.

*Is that true of St. Paul's High School too?*

No, I think St. Paul's still has a pretty strong boarding section, but certainly the number of students from the area has grown there since the area has grown so much and there's such a demand for education, for schools in the area. They're actually turning people away now. Back in the 1960s, students from Mandeville, Madisonville, Folsom, all came to Covington for high school.

*I'm glad to hear you tell of how the schools have developed along with the community. I've been looking at Walker Percy as less an academician and literary artist than as an actual person in the community. Some of what I've picked up has been very interesting. He seems to have been a devoted citizen. He also has the essay he wrote on the "holiness of the ordinary." I wanted to ask if you thought that Catholicism gave him an entrance into this holiness of the ordinary that other codes and systems he had been exposed to did not.*

It's certainly possible, especially considering how his best descriptions are reminiscent of Gerard Manley Hopkins. And, as it's known, he did suffer somewhat from depression, and he had to deal with the whole idea of depression and the suicides in his family. Most probably Catholicism nourished whatever was there. The whole idea of the incarnation of knowledge, of God present, of God's being reflected in others, the idea of the physical body of Christ, all point to that idea of the holiness of the ordinary. The body of Christ that nobody talks about very much in Catholic theology now, but it was talked about a lot in the fifties and the sixties. After that, it became one of those things that Catholics don't focus on as much as they used to.

Percy, being the man he was, would've been familiar with that theology and very much familiar with the similar theology of Flannery O'Connor. As you read Flannery O'Connor's *Habit of Being* and look at all of the different theologians she was reading, it's all pre-Vatican II. He would've been reading a lot of the same people, and there was a lot of this idea of the physical body of Christ then, incarnational theology, and I would imagine that it had something to do with it. I don't know, as I never spoke with him about that.

When I did have conversations with him, they were mostly on more practical things. Walker's daughters, Mary Pratt and then Anne, came to our school. Walker served on the school board and also served as an impromptu consultant to us, I believe in 1969, when there was a problem with St. Peter's School. At the time, the principal, who was one of our sisters, felt that the black people were being discriminated against, that policies were being set up at the parish level for admission to school that made it impossible for black people to qualify. We broached the subject with our pastor, and he got very irate, and I went and had a talk with Walker. A couple of meetings were set up between the pastor and his council and some of the sisters and Walker Percy. That's the sort of thing Walker could help advise us on. What we ended up doing in that case was withdrawing our sisters from the school because we really felt in the end that there was an injustice going on, so we withdrew and didn't staff the school. Years later, things changed and some of our sisters went back there. Walker was very active, in a quiet way but in a determined way, about civil rights and about the black population in Covington.

*Were the public schools integrated at that time?*

Oh yes, this was the late sixties, and the public schools were integrated already. I think there were still some tensions, it hadn't all been smoothed out in the schools. There were also still some tensions between the white community and the black. Other sisters were more active in those changes. I had been away until 1969, and I stepped right back into the middle of things.

*How well did you know Walker? Were you familiar enough with him to discuss spiritual matters or his work?*

No, I wouldn't say I was that close. I knew him well enough to go to his house to consult with him, to call him on the phone about practical matters. When I was superior of the community, I called him once and asked him if he would come. We had an idea that what we needed to do was get some outside people, not other sisters but some good Catholics, and have them live with us a bit to evaluate our work. We wanted a perspective on how they saw us, what might be good for us to do, to give us a layman's view of how we might direct our activities. So I called him about the idea, and he said, "Oh, no, I couldn't do that. Now if you can get me in that monastery over there, I'd like to do that. But no, I really couldn't do that." He was, I wouldn't say shy, but rather reticent. There was nothing pompous about Walker Percy.

He called me once when the Eucharistic Sisters of St. Dominic out here were trying to donate a piece of property to be used for a housing development for the black community. In order for the grant to go through, they needed it to be incorporated into the city. On that occasion, Walker called and asked me to go to a meeting to fight for the incorporation, which I did, but we didn't succeed. The city would not incorporate that property. The property is still there and it's still vacant, but I believe it's finally been incorporated, but it's going to be turned into a park.

Walker was very active in such things. Our relationship was more on a business level. But he evidently admired our group. He worked closely with Sister Jeanette. He named—was it Val who became a sister in *The Last Gentleman*? When she takes her vows, she is going to take the name of Sister Jeanette. And he also admired the Eucharistic Missionary Sisters. He has a religious community in that book, and it's a play on the same name. It was more of a collegial kind of relationship that he had with the sisters.

Our contact as a religious community with Walker Percy goes back to when he first moved to Covington. When he and Bunt first moved to Covington—this would've been in the early fifties—there was a sister who was staying with us and working with our community, but she was from a community in Kansas where Sister Jeanette is now. I was a student at that time in St. Scholastica. This sister, Mary Teresa Brentano, had a doctorate in English and had published some Catholic English literature books, and she had taught at Catholic University. She was a creative person, an idea person, a very delightful and intelligent person. She was very successful in our getting a grant to establish the first classrooms to teach with tapes. That was when the whole idea of tape teaching was new. Of course, it's gone by the wayside now, but it was the latest technology at the time. But I remember that somehow she knew about Walker Percy, and he wasn't published yet. He and Bunt had moved from New Orleans, and one Sunday afternoon, Sister Mary Teresa and the superior at the time took some of us girls to go visit Walker Percy at his house. That was before he lived where he does now, at another place in Covington. Sister Mary Teresa was still in enough contact with the people in the literary world, who said to her that there was a writer in Covington, even though he hadn't been published yet. So we went to his house that Sunday afternoon, and I have an early recollection of meeting Dr. and Mrs. Percy, but little did I know when I was a teenager how important that meeting would be.

I recall that Walker and Bunt, for many years, helped to pay the tuition for a black student to go to St. Scholastica.

*Was it an open scholarship?*

Yes. We would find the student, and they would not know who was paying their tuition. We were trying to integrate the school, which was difficult when you had a black community that couldn't afford tuition.

*Is there a sizable population of black Catholics in the area?*

I don't have a number, but I know that they're a small minority. In New Orleans, though, in some areas the black Catholics outnumber the white Catholics.

*Was it a very bold move for the sisters to withdraw from St. Peter's?*

Oh, yes. We had taught at St. Peter's School since its inception, and St. Scholastica, St. Peter's Church, and the school were right next to each other. The school was in the convent's backyard. It was an extremely bold move for us to take, and it didn't endear us to a lot of the older Covington people who had had children there or who still had children there. It did make a statement, but how effective it was, I don't know.

*Did you see a tension in Percy's involvement with the sisters' work versus his involvement with the Benedictine order here? Your order has always been very involved with the community, and the monastic community seems to be more about retreat.*

He seemed to fit closer to Benedictine life than he did to being in the thick of a battle. He was a retiring kind of man, not the type to push himself in any direction. Sometimes we think of movements being led by very strident people who must fight for justice and get it all done by six o'clock. He was anything but that. It was easier to see him in a more contemplative, quiet stance than an active stance. But he was both. There is no doubt his action was fortified by his contemplation and his faith, and because of that he could approach the movements or the causes without bitterness and he could maintain his own inner calm. But I'm sure it cost him something any time he had to be a public person, so to speak, instead of being involved with things literary.

Regarding things literary, I remember once when Dr. Percy was asked to talk to a senior English class at St. Paul's School. He was finishing *The Second Coming* at the time, and I went along. He really wasn't giving a lecture, he was more talking informally, and the students would ask questions. He was asked about the book he was working on, and I remember that a student asked him, "Well, how is it going to turn out?" And he said, "I don't know. It's not finished yet." And the student couldn't understand that. She said, "You mean you haven't planned how it's going to end?" and he said, "No, I have to just wait and see what these characters are going to do." The students had a hard time believing that he wrote that way.

But I'm glad to have known Walker Percy personally, at least a little bit. I always found him to be a gentleman, a southern Catholic gentleman, a real gallant.

# Judy LaCour, Teacher
COVINGTON, LOUISIANA

*Judy LaCour taught English and drama to seniors for a number of years at St. Paul's School in Covington. Located very near the Percy home, St. Paul's is a Catholic LaSallian school, part of the mission of the Brothers of the Christian Schools, commonly referred to as the Christian Brothers. The school is staffed by both brothers and lay-persons. LaCour now serves as director of development and alumni relations for the school. She knew Walker Percy as a neighbor and friend, and Percy made special visits to her classes to discuss literature and his career on a number of occasions. She spoke about Percy from the Dakota Restaurant in Covington.*

I knew Walker more as a citizen. He came to my classes for a number of years to speak with my students. We became acquainted when I first went to St. Paul's. My very first year there, I put on a play called *Montage of Time*, and it had some very strong, very controversial statements. It was written by a man over in New Orleans who was a friend, one of the people who wrote *Hair*. He used much of their technique and much of their music to put together this thing. It was a strong statement on race relations, on the war—this was in 1969 and 1970. I put this on, and it was very popular. It was the first time in Covington—maybe one of the first times in Louisiana—that black and white actors had appeared on a school stage together. I invited black students from the Covington High area, Covington and Mandeville, and we put on the play. It was a very strong statement. It used a collage technique in presentation. At that time, I really didn't know who Walker Percy was. He came and brought his daughter, and she just fell in love with the play. They came back several times, and he wrote me a fan note. I was very pleased with that, of course, but I didn't know who he was and I didn't save it. Can you believe that?

Anyway, he wrote me the note, and at that time Dr. Percy was very active in trying to end racial prejudice here in Covington.

Emily Diamond and Brother Paul from our school, along with Walker, started the first credit union for black people here. Until that time, there was nothing that would provide money for blacks who needed it. But he wrote me a highly complimentary note and indicated that he felt the play was making real inroads to combating racism in Covington. The problem was severe. One of our leading citizens was openly a Klan member.

Dr. Percy had very strong feelings. One would have thought that he was a "damn Yankee," which of course he was not. He was very much a southerner. But so far as Covington was concerned, he was an outsider, an agitator, Yankee, whatever. Through the credit union, Dr. Percy and the others were trying to put an end to some of the social handicaps of being black.

*Has it changed very much now?*

Oh, yes. I don't hesitate to say so. I thank Habitat for Humanity for continuing that work. Also, I'm a member of the First Baptist Church in Covington. I joined when I first came here in the sixties, and it was all-white and proud of it. There were some deacons in the church during this period who had such a fear that some of the blacks would come in and sit down in the church that they already had a plan to get up and walk out if it happened. Now this isn't universal in our church. Now we have black members, and the church is supporting financially a program called Second Chance for people who are coming out of jail and need a fresh start. Just in that small instance it shows you that some things have changed. Maybe the community as a whole has not come far enough, but some things are better. But when I first was at St. Paul's, we had to cancel a speech and banquet scheduled for the country club because they found that members of my group were black. It has come a long way, yes. Does it need to go further? Of course. I think that in many ways that attitudes in Covington are more open-minded than some of the attitudes in other towns that I have visited.

Dr. Percy not only took this responsibility, he lived it. He was very open about his beliefs, and I also know that he helped people financially. I happen to know that because I know some of the people he helped, but I also know that he remained anonymous in cases like that. Everything he did, if possible, was anonymous because he was not at all, in fact he would be the last person in the world to want credit for what he did.

I used to tease him about *Lancelot*, which is my least favorite of his books. I was in Albuquerque, New Mexico, once, about to get on a plane and needing something to read. If you've seen the cover of the early paperback copy of *Lancelot*, it has this very seductive-looking woman leaning over, with a priest standing in the back, and I just burst out laughing. People who didn't know, who picked it up and read it, probably were shocked because it wasn't like Harold Robbins. So anyway, I came home and I teased him, saying that he'd made the big time because he had seminude women on his book cover. He was appalled, just appalled, that people would think of him in terms of trying for popularity that way. Heaven knows, if you're familiar with his books, that was not his thing.

When he and I first became friendly, I hadn't read any of his books. *The Moviegoer* had just won the National Book Award and I got a copy and I hated it. I mean, I literally hated it. I must admit that I attempted to read it two or three times before I made it through to the end. But when he did *The Last Gentleman*, my favorite of all his books, I thought that he had a great deal to say. That was when I invited him to meet with my honors English class, and he did. Well, the kids did not know who he was either, and they didn't appreciate it because I was always dragging somebody in there. But this kept going for a while, and then later, when a class of mine studied *Love in the Ruins*, he came to my class. That must've been maybe 1973. I was giving a seminar that year because I had some students who were much too bright for the regular honors class. I chose the top ten or eleven students and made a separate class for them. I remember scheduling Dr. Percy for a conference with us, and when he came, my students had read *Love in the Ruins*, and at the time we were discussing the theme of how violent things were. We were talking and Dr. Percy started throwing out questions to them. This is the way he taught. This man never lectured at students. He was just sitting up there, asking them, "What do you think about this?" and "What do you think about that?" and the students were just popping off answers. You could see the amazement on Dr. Percy's face. He stayed after class and said, "Judy, I have to tell you something. I'm teaching a college class right now, and I feel like taking your students with me and letting them show my students how to talk." It was an exceptional class. But after that I never had difficulty getting him to come to my class, and he became a kind of tradition, and the kids learned that they were getting something special.

Well, this last class was sitting with him, and they had read *The Thanatos Syndrome*, and they were talking about death. I think that by then, Walker was already aware of his illness, very aware of his mortality, and the kids were really talking with him. And he'd be asking them, "What do you think, what do you think?" and then they turned it on him and asked him what he thought about something. He told them, "I don't read that stuff. Once I write it, it's written, and I don't read it again. I don't know what I was thinking when I wrote that."

Let me tell you, the approach that he used totally changed me as a teacher. What happened is, prior to that class, I was the typical English teacher who got all the answers from the teacher's guidebook for every piece of literature. After getting to know Dr. Percy and listening to him talk with my students that day, I changed my approach. Basically, what he said was that writing a piece of literature was like giving birth to a baby. You knew what you would like for it to be and you hoped it would become what you wanted, but you never could be sure because there were all kinds of influences, by the person who had given birth to it, by other people he had come in contact with, and by the reader. He said, "You know, I can't tell you what it means. It means what it means to you. There are sometimes I can't even tell you what it means to me. At the moment, it seemed the appropriate thing to write. That's one of the reasons that I don't want to go back and re-read anything because maybe at another day, at another time, it would have been different."

This touched me deeply because it made me so unsure of these English class "truths" that I'd been teaching. I started approaching my teaching as he did, that is say, "Let's look at it, let's look at the clues that are there, let's look at the influences that might have touched this person consciously or unconsciously, let's look at it in different ways." I just became absolutely a different teacher.

*I had heard some earlier comments that Percy wasn't comfortable in the classroom. I'm surprised to hear that he was so successful.*

He was incredible. It was just that he was so intent on sharing. I won't say sharing his vision because I never got a sense that he was trying to push across a point of view, but I knew from talking to him that he did not believe in preaching through literature. Sometimes people said that he meant to push a lesson in his writing. There were themes, surely, multiple themes, but I don't think he cared about whether someone took it or not. He wasn't pushing.

In that last class meeting before he died, though, they had been having a very intense discussion about all of the themes in *The Thanatos Syndrome* and the problems in the world, and how he'd painted such a dark picture. Somebody asked him if he thought there was any hope. It makes me cry when I remember this because I am fairly certain he knew at the time that he was about to die. He said, "We had our chance. We old guys, we had our chance." Then he put his hands out to them and said, "This is where the hope lies, with you guys. We had our chance and we blew it."

You don't necessarily see a lot of hope in *The Thanatos Syndrome*. We have a plaque in the school now with a picture of Dr. Percy and his little dog on it, and every year the outstanding English student receives an award and has his name added to it. We quoted him on the plaque. At the bottom it says, "This is where the hope lies." He felt that for people who read, who thought, who understood what's happening to us as human beings, that there was hope.

I'm sixty-five now and soon I'll retire, and I miss being in the classroom. I'm at an age now where I am very serious about teaching, but I don't have the energy for the preparation that I used to have. I don't mean to be one of the older generation defying the power of the younger generation, but I find that there are fewer and fewer young people, even the bright young people, who seem to care about reading, and thinking, and searching for answers. They would like very much to walk in and open their mouths and let you just throw it into them so they can regurgitate it.

*Sort of like "The Thanatos Syndrome"?*

Right. Exactly. I don't want to teach that way. I can't teach that way.

Walker made too much of a difference in my life. He told me that if you can't make them think, then you've wasted your time.

*It sounds like he's still very much with you.*

He is, he is. You know, I still have difficulty with that. He remains very alive to me.

# Lee Barrios, Former Assistant
ABITA SPRINGS, LOUISIANA

*Lee Barrios, formerly Lee Binnings, served Walker Percy as typist and editor for several years. She is a teacher now and lives with her husband, Wayne, outside Abita Springs. There are horses outside, and the floors of her house are antique heart pine, with nail holes in them from a past life when they were part of another structure. Her home is in the country, and it's just as comfortable as can be.*

Walker seemed very concerned about what people thought about what he wrote. When he gave me the draft of *The Second Coming*, he was especially concerned about a particular character, I think it was the chicken man. He was concerned because he knew at the time that I was really heavy-duty into the Bible, and he didn't know me that well at all. He needed a typist, and my husband had said that his wife does that, so he hired me. He called me because he hadn't heard from me after he gave me the manuscript. It was half handwriting, half typed. So he called me and asked if I was alright or if I was having any problems. I said no, not at all, and he said, "Well, I hope you're not embarrassed by any of the characters in there." And I wasn't. I thought that was funny. He would show up at my door—I had sort of a balcony with French doors where I typed—and he'd knock on the door, open the door, and say, "Lee, having any problems?" He had a little bit of a stutter, he was a very shy person. He reminded me a lot of my dad. I remember in the book he had a character who was supposed to be a Jehovah's Witness, so I asked him when I was through typing the book whether I could talk to him about the book. And I think he was thinking, "Oh my gosh," fearing that I was going to have something to say about it and have to retype it or rework it. That's what he did, evidently, if people complained or they had a problem with something, he just felt really concerned about it. So I asked him, I just mentioned that the Jehovah's Witness is not a typical Jehovah's Witness, and if you want it to be a typical Jehovah's Witness, here's what you need to know. The next thing I know is the book was published and the character was a Baptist.

*Wow. Did he let a lot of people see his work in progress?*

No, no. I heard that he did not want people reading it because he responded personally and philosophically that way, so I don't think he let people see it for that reason.

When I told him that I had gone back to school, I told him that I was taking a linguistics course, Linguistics for Non-Linguists. And I wrote him a note that I had to correspond with somebody about a linguistics subject. So I told the professor that maybe I would read *Message in a Bottle* and get Walker to respond to my thoughts about it. The professor thought that would be great. So I wrote Walker a letter and asked him if I read the book and wrote him a response to it, would he either write back and say I was crazy or comment in any kind of way. So he wrote back and said sure, whatever I wanted, he'd be glad to do it. The first letter was very short, and the second letter was very long. I didn't realize that *Message in a Bottle* was so involved. It's not a book for beginners. So I delved a little bit into the philosophy, which I know very little about, and sent him the letter. The next thing I knew, I got a phone call from Walker, and he asked, "Lee, did you get my response to your letter?" I hadn't, and he said, "Oh, I think I sent it to the wrong address. Would you try to track it down because I'd hate to have to write it all over again." Well, I didn't realize how sick he was, and he died a month later. He had sent it to the wrong address, and I could not track it down, so I never got the letter.

He at one point said, when he was typing his second book—he typed on a typewriter and then handwrote about half of it—that Bunt had bought him a word processor and that he was scared to death of it. He was trying to learn to use it. I do have that note from him.

He was very unassuming. He had an office at the top of the spiral staircase at the top of the bookstore [the Kumquat, run by Percy's daughter, which is no longer in business]. People would occasionally go visit him, but I don't think people really bothered him. I think that's why he liked this area. People knew who he was and they appreciated him personally, but they let him be. There are people outside here who seemed to worship him. He was an icon. It was amazing to me how many people I've heard say he was a prophet.

*Would you tell more about when you first met him and when you first started working on his manuscripts and reading his stories?*

When I first met him, my husband was the starving-artist type and was going to these luncheons with a group of other artists and writers and friends. Rhoda Faust was one of them, Bob Milling, others. So my husband referred me to him for typing, and he called me and then brought me a manuscript. I didn't know who he was. I'd had two years of college, was raising kids and riding horses. So he brought me the manuscripts, and I didn't look at them at first from a reader's or a philosophical standpoint. But it was very interesting to me. His characterizations were what I really enjoyed.

*What sort of man did he seem to be when you met him?*

Like I said, he reminded me a lot of my dad. My dad looked kind of like him, and my dad was a very introspective person who was very opinionated, and when you got him really stirred up, he'd respond to you. Walker was the very same way, except very low-key and quiet. He did sit me down once when I gave him one of his manuscripts, though, and he asked me what I thought of his books. That's when I told him about the Jehovah's Witness character. I couldn't believe later that I said that. I couldn't believe that he asked me.

*What was your favorite book?*

I'd say *The Second Coming*, but of course that was the first book I worked on for him. To me, the characters were real people. They were out there, like in all of his books. But as I was typing, I felt like I was into the actual story, the action. They were just so common, way out there but common. I guess that comes from my family. I have these typical strange southern relations, so nothing was strange to me. The insanity and the eccentricity of the characters seemed normal to me. I think it is normal—if you're not crazy, then you're boring. Who are you? You're nobody.

Here's a letter he wrote after I had finished a manuscript in 1982: "Thanks. You make it look better than it is. How do you expect good sense from a novelist? I confess that sometimes I have to laugh when I think of you reading my stuff and knowing what a strong-minded lady you are and your strong convictions, to imagine your reaction: 'Where does he get those dumb ideas? I'd like to straighten him out. I'd like to tell him a thing or two.' Right? All the best, Walker."

That's really the way he thought. He thinks that of everybody, that folks don't know what to make of him.

*Was he prone to periods of depression?*

I didn't know him well enough to say.

*There has been some mention before of his suffering from depression, but I've also heard from others that he occasionally was full of compulsive energy that sounds almost manic at times.*

I could believe that. It was almost like you couldn't tell by Walker's words what he was thinking, but you could see. You could just look at Walker, and you could tell that he was thinking, definitely. He was always puttering around in that old truck, and he was always having lunches and meetings with people. I wouldn't say he was depressive all the time. I would say he had hyper spurts. He wasn't verbal about it, but under his skin I think he was. His stuttering, whether it was actually a stutter, maybe a stammer, was like that. It was a lot like my dad—you knew that he was really thinking about something. He was not going to just come out and say anything off the top of his head, but he was very straightforward and honest.

Like a lot of my gifted students, it seems that he thought faster than he could verbalize. To me, I would guess that writing for him was painful almost. I don't know what he's told people in interviews. You can tell from his handwriting. When I look at my gifted kids' writing—they think fast, so their writing is terrible, you can't read it, but you can tell by what they do get down on paper that there's a whole lot in there and that they understand. But if you were grading it strictly grammatically, it wouldn't be good. That's the impression I got about Walker. His writing was probably a release to him. He couldn't release verbally, but through these characters.

*I've heard that he revised his work over and over.*

I think he did. I always wondered. He'd have me type it and then give me revisions two or three times, and I suspected that the work had been revised lots more times before I got the changes and before it ever got published. He seemed to compose on the typewriter and make his revisions by hand.

*Did he ever just sit down and get you to talk, to see what you'd have to
say?*

Just that one time that I told you about, with his book. I think that
he did sense that I was very curious about the same thing that he
was curious about, the source of spirituality and that kind of thing.
I never sat down with him like that, though. I'd be interested to
know whether he wanted to have that kind of conversation with me
or not. I don't know who he enjoyed talking from the heart with—
the priest types or his close friends, people who did agree with him,
people who didn't, or what. I didn't get that opportunity.

I mentioned in my introduction at a dinner a few years ago that
he wasn't somebody who had all the answers, but he did have all
the questions. That's the way he was, that Socratic type. He wasn't
trying to teach, he was trying to find out your viewpoint. I think
you could read his books millions of times and still get something
new out of it.

I often thought after he died that he was a tragic character. Then
several years later my dad died, and they were very much alike in a
way. His death was tragic too. I had the same question about both
of them: Did Walker die still not knowing? What was it like on his
deathbed? I picture him thinking, "Oh my gosh, I don't know the
answer, I really haven't devised an answer for myself, but I'm about
to find out the hard way."

The same thing goes for my dad. He had never made his peace
—he fought in the war and he killed all these people in Korea
and Vietnam, and he never could reconcile that. He couldn't ex-
press it. It made me sad that somebody would go out that way, and
whether it was that way for Walker or not, I don't know, but I got
that sense.

Yet it's good too because there are so many people that decide
they have the answer, and they're satisfied and that's it for them.
Of course, they don't have the answer, and they don't even live as if
they have the answer. It's something that doesn't bother me at all.
For me, there is no answer until you actually experience it, whatever it is, life after death, whatever. That doesn't bother me. It's
just a challenge. I got the sense from Walker that he felt like it was
very important, and he would have liked to know whether he had
the answer, whether he was doing what was right, whether he was

living out the life that he should. He expressed that through all his characters.

I felt like he was in his stories, and I wonder how he came up with these people because they seemed so real to him. Some of the things they did were so strange.

*Like what?*

Like Binx Bolling and some of his thoughts. I would think, "Yeah, I can see that, and that's weird. Am I weird too?"

I really enjoyed reading his books. I had the same feeling the first time I read Updike. I wrote a comparative paper on *Run, Rabbit, Run* and *The Moviegoer*. It's been a while now since I did, but the comparisons between Updike and Walker are very clear to me. It was so much like Walker—always this comic character, a priest.

*Based on what you've said, did you ever wonder why he was drawn to Catholicism, why he converted?*

He talked to me a little bit about that. He said that it was the ceremony that he liked at first. That's what a lot of people say about the Catholic church, I know, but I think that was a big draw for him, all the tradition, and the ceremony, and the pomp and circumstance. Now from my experience teaching and seeing my kids and their responses to art and music and poetry, I see now that there's an innate spirituality there. A lot of kids these days know nothing about religion. Half of them don't even go to church, yet they will respond in a very spiritual way to these things. I think that Walker got that sense from the Catholic church. I don't know if it was just the art and music in itself, though, or something more.

*Did your reading Percy's works affect your own search?*

Yes, later, after I had gone back to school and earned a master's and reflected on the experience and read his stuff again. I've always felt like that kind of person who always has the questions, not the answers, and I don't think we'll ever know in this lifetime. That's what I liked about his writing, the constant "I wonder who I am," and how everything you experience is part of the solution to the problem, seeing it that way instead of as just another event in your life, another day went by. To me it's an experience, something you saw, something you did, something you ate, it's all part of a big picture. I think that's the way he saw it.

His characterizations were always that way. They were so simple, yet he would point out things that other writers wouldn't, that would be too simple or unimportant. But he'd bring that out and you could visualize his character, you thought you knew the character based on those few little things. I remember the girl in *The Second Coming* by the weight of her hair, how it had something to do with her as a person.

*Do you think he ever became comfortable with having so many unanswered questions?*

I have to think that for him it was like the guy who climbs Mt. Everest. Whether he conquers it or not, it's the challenge. That's what life is all about, that's what's interesting. I see my kids in school, and they're convinced that if they get an A, that's where it's at. No concept whether they learned anything or how hard they had to work for it, just "Did I get an A?" They don't understand that attempting to reach the A, that's where it's at, that's the thrill. To them, that's just work, but I think for Walker, that's where it's at.

You figure if you have all the answers, how boring can that be? And then you have to live with your answer, which means you have to justify that your answer is a good thing and that it's correct. What do you do if you get the answers?

There are no answers in Catholicism. Do you think Catholics have the answer? Don't they say everything's a mystery? I think he loved the mystery in it. And I know I've said that in some ways I didn't know him that well, but I think I did know him. I knew him through his books. And he was a great writer, to me, because the message got through.

I think that the people who are into his work are people who look at life. I would think that they would be people who are insightful and curious yet don't think they have any answers. Not ultraconservative types, but people who are reading just to get in touch with themselves.

What makes me curious about Walker is that he was trained as a doctor and intended to be a psychiatrist. That's clinical—here are some cells, and that's why you do what you do and think what you think. But Walker, I don't see how he ever made it through that because he looks at life from the philosophical and the spiritual. To me the spiritual is totally different from the clinical, and you can't explain that part of you clinically. Psychiatrists, I think, try to explain everything you do from a clinical standpoint. That was curious about him.

*Makes you wonder what sort of manner he would've had if he had practiced.*

He would've been on the couch, I'm sure, and as you were asking him questions, he'd have been asking you questions.

*You mentioned earlier that you got to know him through the group of artists and writers he met with. How did he appear in that group?*

Well, ever since I met my ex-husband in college, I've been exposed to nothing but artist and philosopher types. Out of all the artists I've met, maybe a handful were what I would call serious thinkers. Most of them were just symbolically artists—they walk the walk and talk the talk. Walker didn't do that. I don't think he even had to repress himself to keep from doing that. He'd sit and listen, and when those people got together at lunch, their conversation—without saying anything, he kept them from being the overt, typical artist type. They thought before they said anything to him. They didn't ask him silly questions. They talked about things that happened in their everyday lives, and they couldn't help but get on the subject of literature and philosophy and those sorts of things, but it was very low-key. Very few artists that I've met were real like Walker. I can't imagine any pretension getting past Walker.

The group, including Walker, would discuss whether they were going to allow somebody to participate in their luncheon. The people that were questionable were the ones who tried to show themselves as artists, tried to be the artist type and talk too much, that sort of thing. Sometimes they would have some well-known people, some famous actors and writers, visit them. I remember once that there was one British actor who came, well-known but I forget his name, and he was the very serious type, and his wife was a real flit. The guys in the lunch group were like a bunch of little old women, talking about these people after they'd gone. It was funny. I think Walker enjoyed that. There was nothing phony about him at all.

I wonder if he was afraid that he'd fall into that pit. He was so revered, it would have been easy for him to walk around conceited like that. Maybe he was afraid that would happen to him, like some people are afraid they might go crazy for no clear reason. He really did keep away from that sort of thing. He was asked to give a lot of speeches, but he was very picky about who he would speak to. He would speak to maybe a third-grade class or a fund-raiser for locals, for example, and turn down a graduation speech at a university.

I think that's why he drove the vehicle he drove. Everybody knew it was Walker. That was his trademark, that old, beat-up, crummy little truck. He'd drive around hunched over, no air-conditioning, no nothing, in that little vehicle.

*Speaking of pretense, I was approached after a conference once by an academic who has a theory that Walker wrote "A Confederacy of Dunces" as an experiment and fabricated the whole story of O'Toole. She had no reason, no proof, to support her ideas. I asked her why, and she said, "I just think so."*

Something like that would make Walker absolutely die if he heard it. I can just hear him saying, "People really think that? Oh my God!" That's what he was all about—the ordinary. And he really worked at being ordinary and maintaining it. I think that's where he thought the source of spirituality, or the answer, or the true self, was: somewhere ordinary. He was so highly educated, but it seemed that maybe he was thinking he'd never find himself. It was like Binx Bolling—the more he thought about it, the more involved he got, the more he was losing himself. Life was getting really complicated. I think maybe Walker had that feeling.

# Rhoda Faust, Bookshop Owner

NEW ORLEANS, LOUISIANA

*Rhoda Faust spoke about Walker Percy at a coffee shop near her book-store, the Maple Street Book Shop, just off St. Charles Avenue in New Orleans. Maple Street is one of the smaller, independent bookstores that readers fall in love with for its charm as well as its excellent selection. There are photographs of Percy in the bookstore, some including Faust. Faust, who has always lived in New Orleans, first came to know Percy through his brother Phin's friendship with her father. In later years, she became a regular in Percy's Thursday lunch group across Lake Pontchartrain. There is an extensive collection of Percy's books in the shop, including books signed by Percy at autograph parties at the store. When asked whether she would grant an interview about Walker Percy, she responded in the same spirit as many others, stating that she was "happy to help with anything that keeps Walker's memory alive."*

When my mother and my aunt started the store in 1964, I worked part-time in the afternoons now and then as a high school student, which amounted mostly to me demanding money for snacks and going on cigarette breaks. In 1971 I took over from my mother, who had already taken over from my aunt. I was in my early twenties. We're close to Tulane, Loyola, and Dominican, not too far from Xavier. At that point we did more class orders than we do now. There were a lot of counterculture professors who would make a point of ordering from us to boycott their schools' own operations.

*Do you remember any stories about your father and his friendship with Dr. Percy?*

My father, Lee, was in one of Walker's lunch groups, his "geriatric" group, as Walker used to say, that met on Wednesdays. My father and mother were also in one of the Great Books groups in Covington. And they would correspond. They felt somewhat politically different. My father's politically conservative, and Walker, at that time in particular, was more liberal politically, so sometimes they would correspond about some issue that had been in the papers. Also they were both doctors, so there was that tie. They weren't ever big buddies, though. I think one of the things that Walker found interesting about my father and maybe, therefore, about me is that my father's so different from Walker. My father's very structured, very strict, literal, and I don't want to say noncreative, but he has a surgeon's personality as opposed to a writer's. It seems like they were worlds apart. Walker liked my father, and I think Walker found my father interesting in that he was so different.

Walker remembered a story about first meeting me when I was seven. My father and all the kids went over to Walker and Bunt's house. When we got there, my father started asking me if I had brushed my teeth that morning. I told him that I didn't, and he sent me with Walker to go to the bathroom and brush my teeth. My father was very strict. Walker reminded me twenty years later of that, saying it was something he never would have done as a father. He said he was interested in that father-daughter interchange, and how it struck him as being so different from himself. He wanted to know why I was asked, why I said yes, and so on. He always wanted to know things like that.

*At what point did you get to know Walker as a novelist and not just as a friend of the family?*

I remember that Walker was coming into the bookshop right after my mother opened it. *The Moviegoer* came out around that same time, and my mother was a big supporter of his. He was coming to the bookshop to sign books, and I'd see him there. Later I was part of another one of Walker's Great Books groups, a separate one from my parents. When I took over the bookshop in 1970, he offered to do signings for some of his other books. I thought it was fabulous. It was a reason for us to be corresponding and talking on the phone, and it was symbiotic. He wanted his books to sell and get out there into the world.

At that point he wasn't as hesitant to have signings and be among the people. I think money was an issue for him at that time, with a deaf child. Anne was on the scene, and he had to pay for operations. He would help me promote by attending signings and sometimes letting me drive over to Covington with boxes of books for him to sign. So we did business together, and that put me in a special category. It was legit, but it was also fun for me to be getting to know him better and forming a friendship.

*You said that he wasn't hesitant to do book signings "at that point." Did he become reluctant about that later?*

It got to the point where he found autograph parties too embarrassing. He'd forget names, and he'd be on display, and his natural shyness would just make him suffer. Later he would still do that for Anne at her bookstore, but for us he wouldn't have a party where he'd have to see people. His publisher was trying to get him to go on tours later as well, but he hated those nationwide tours.

*When did you first pick up one of his books and read it?*

My mother got me to read *The Moviegoer* pretty soon after it came out. I was nineteen or twenty. I didn't get it. I liked it, but more because it was nice that somebody I knew wrote it. I thought it was interesting at that age, but not as interesting as some. It wasn't overtly racy or profane. I was reading raunchier stuff, but I was also reading Camus and Sartre.

What it boils down to is that it took me three readings of *The Moviegoer* to realize he was being funny. I simply just didn't get it. He had to tell me. One day he asked me about *The Moviegoer*, and I said, "Well, I like it, but it was kind of slow." I was trying to be honest. And he said, "Well, you know it's supposed to be funny." I didn't realize that. He wasn't a laugh a minute in person, even though he was good-spirited. Thank God. Once knowing he was trying to be funny, I read it for the third time and I just loved it. From then on, I knew to look for the humor. You would think I would have known it anyway. Discovering his sort of humor made me love everything he wrote after that. Too bad I needed help, but I did.

*I've noticed that deadpan humor and irony like Percy's slips by students very easily.*

Well, I was also adolescent at that point, very troubled, and drunk, and guilty-feeling, and wanting to be serious, reading lots of serious stuff, may have done it. I didn't know that I was allowed to find some stuff funny, that it was okay to be satirical. I took the New Orleans party line about families and society and what's expected. I was rejecting the whole Catholic thing at that time.

*Do you consider yourself to be a Catholic now?*

I'm a recently returned Catholic—lapsed—and that feels great. Walker had a powerful influence on me in that area. I'd go around with a whole lot of scoffers, and the fact that Walker was so venerated, to use some hyperbole, revered. He's brilliant and he believes in Jesus Christ, and he made the leap of faith or whatever it is that made him a true believer. That's what it boils down to.

*Did you get a sense that he ever really found answers or that he was comfortable with answers that he had found?*

I remember asking him something like "Do you really believe that Jesus Christ was the son of God and that he came down to save the world, and therefore we are saved?" My emphasis was really on whether Walker believed that Jesus was the son of God. He didn't give me an unequivocal "yes." His response was more like a "Well, that's what I am choosing." It was enough of a yes. He wasn't trying to say, "I am certain about it," but he was saying that "I am choosing to believe in it. I am buying into it. I am going to Mass. It is what I want." That was sufficient for me. He didn't use Pascal's wager or anything like that—it wasn't cynical whatsoever. I know that he and Bunt walked to Mass a lot of afternoons, and it was real for him.

I wish that he were still around to talk to now that I went back, just in the last eight or ten months.

*That recently? What prompted you to go back?*

I had other friends that I respected who'd come back. But Walker was the first one who made me think, "Wait. Hold it. For twenty-five years I've been away. I need to pay more attention. Maybe I'm on the wrong track after all, being away from church."

He got me interested, but then it took me being friends with a nun who'd had a mental breakdown who was down here for therapy. Alright, so I go to therapy. So I got to know her, and I really respect her spirituality, her assurance, her utter faith and comfort and belief. She articulated it more than Walker ever did. So she and a few more friends helped me come to a realization, and I feel safe around them to start believing also. I've started going to Mass with a friend and confession, communion—I'm back. I feel very glad about that.

I'm doing my best not to be a smorgasbord Catholic and to buy into the whole thing. I'm sort of making my way. It's hard to say that Jesus is the only way to God. I don't understand that exactly, but I'm on my way to buying the whole thing. That doesn't sound good. It sounds arrogant, but too bad.

I remember that right around the time Walker and I were talking about whether he really believed, that I had heard this gospel tape. I went out and bought him a copy of it—it was Reverend Barnes and Sister Brown or Reverend Brown and Sister Barnes, I can't remember. It was black gospel music, and the lead song was "What More Do You Want Him to Do?" It was about God sending his son, who died on the cross, you know the story. What other sign are you waiting for? What else do you want?

He said that he listened to the whole tape and that he really liked it and that it was something of a revelation. He asked what I was waiting for. That, to me, was significant. I understood that it was arrogant to think that you need more evidence because you're too smart to buy into this.

*A number of people have remembered Walker for his involvement with civil rights issues in Covington. Did you discuss social issues with him?*

Well, the books themselves supported anti-abortion, thinking and belief. Some folks think the priest in the tower talking about the Nazis in *The Thanatos Syndrome* was a little heavy-handed too, but to me it was just beautifully sound and solid. But that's his writing, as opposed to his actions.

*Which of the books do you like best?*

Of his fiction, I'd say *Thanatos* because I'm more literal, and he was very literal in that book. I knew exactly what he was talking about, and I loved his humor. Also *The Last Gentleman*. My least favorite was *Love in the Ruins*. I don't know why; maybe it's one I need to re-read a time or two. I love *Lost in the Cosmos*. I remember when I read that it transformed my whole day. I'd read five or ten pages every morning and walk out and the world would be different.

It's been ten or twelve years since I read that. It's funny because when I re-read Walker, it's sad. It's just so exciting, and so much better even than the first time I read it because I understand more. I want him to be here so that I can tell him how much I love his books. He would let the lunch group that I was in preview his books sometimes and report back, so I took notes on two or three of them that he gave me and asked for comments. For the most part, what I would do, to make up for not finding *The Moviegoer* funny, was tell him what parts I thought were really funny. He liked hearing that I got his jokes.

I remember that one thing he asked the group about was a short section about "chicken hawks" in the French Quarter of New Orleans—sexual predators. He read it to us and asked if it was too strong or offensive. He was talking about a homosexual chicken hawk in the passage—I don't remember the book it was from. I'm pretty sure, though, that the word he took out was "butt-fuckers" to refer to homosexuals. That would have been pretty strong. There was some anger on his part, I think, at trying to legitimize homosexual behavior, especially when it applied to young kids. I think it was in *The Thanatos Syndrome*. But I know that he became very politically incorrect in some areas, which was part of his version of activism. He didn't take one particular point of view. You just couldn't say that his was a liberal point of view or a conservative point of view. He would be surprising—he would surprise me sometimes. I guess it was his Catholicism kicking in.

*Have any of your perspectives changed since your interviews with Jay Tolson and Patrick Samway?*

Well, my faith has changed—that's a big one. I respect Walker more now and realize more what you're in for if you hold that line, being a Christian and wanting also to be respected for your brain. My respect for Walker has deepened as a result of that. I remember when I was being interviewed by them there were different sorts of questions—this is more fun and loose.

The word "flawed" comes up, but in a good way. As I get older, and having read the biographies, I realize that I was inclined to put Walker on a pedestal. But I had seen some of those flaws, like how he sometimes drank too much, or maybe being approached by and attracted to some of the young women who would try to hang all over him. I know Bunt's aware of that. But his flaws are comforting to me now because I respected his mind so much and his courage to go on in spite of his malaise and his depression. He would talk about his depression, major depression, and physically he didn't feel well a lot of the time. I admire his courage. I think that courage is a big word because he was tormented by temptation in several areas, and he coped with it awfully well. That's what

I'm realizing more and more, that you don't have to be perfect, the way a strict father or the church or nuns say you have to be.

I'm also realizing some of what may have been going on underneath for me was that he was a father figure to some extent, more than just a friend and business partner. Sometimes he'd be sort of flirty, but underneath it he was sometimes fear-filled, he would need to overcome fear to keep going, or the brick wall of depression, which I've never suffered from but he told me so much about it. Other people have told me about it too, who were friends of mine, and it just would have been very tough to have lived his life and also to stay true to his convictions. He knew sometimes that he was going to get massacred by the critics for his books, but he didn't kowtow for his Catholicism, for his belief in God, for his stance on abortion. I think the bit about the chicken hawks was him wanting to make a statement that he didn't think it was right. I read that into what I remember about him, not that he hated homosexuals but that he realized that it wasn't God's plan. God knows that he couldn't have been too overt or it would have ruined his writing. "You can't use a hammer," he'd say, "to make your point. You'll lose people right and left." That was a hard decision for him, to make that opinion felt somewhat without looking like a homophobe.

*Do you remember anything he said about his depression?*

In the context of drinking, he knew that he'd have to limit himself if he wanted to do his work. At lunch he'd have one, sometimes two drinks, but then he'd say that would make him happy. Alcohol would lift that depression for a certain period, but he'd have to limit it.

He was also really proud of being the oldest living Percy, that he'd fought off his depression enough not to commit suicide. That was important to him, that progress, but it was still a constant struggle. I gathered later that suicide was no longer an issue, that Catholicism took that off the table for him. That was something of a relief and another reason that he valued his beliefs.

*Did you have a crush on him when you were so young?*

Yes, I had a lot of affection for him, and probably some unhealthy father-incestuous stuff.

*Now there's a Freudian response.*

I appreciated him valuing me on an equal level. My father lectures
—he is still a father. Walker was like a benign father figure. He
was fatherly, but he was an approving father figure. That felt really
good. He respected my opinions.

*Do you write yourself?*

No, thank God I don't have that urge. I don't have to do that.

*Do you still enjoy reading?*

Oh, yes. I used to be into the existential people, anything that doesn't
just change your view on one or two little things, but whatever
changes the whole picture. To me, that's what Walker did in *Lost in
the Cosmos*. He did that in some of his novels too—they just weren't
a mainline like *Lost in the Cosmos*. I still read classics, contemporary fiction, and mysteries. I love mysteries.

*Do you read Cormac McCarthy?*

I don't. I tried, but on the first page that I got to the Spanish, I thought,
"I don't know Spanish, and if he isn't going to translate this for me,
I'm not going to bother." That was *All the Pretty Horses*. It bugged
me. I probably would love him, but I just haven't been willing to
try again.

    I love Faulkner, utterly love Faulkner. And some of the Germans
—I think I liked Heinrich Boll before I knew Walker did. I once
sent him a new Heinrich Boll, and he told me that I couldn't be
sending him free books or I'd go out of business. I find Boll's *Clown*
and Walker's *The Moviegoer* to be very much alike. Thomas Mann
is really good, and Ian McEwen.

*It's interesting that you mention Faulkner. Comparisons between Percy
and Faulkner seemed to irritate Percy in some interviews that I've
read.*

I just remember loving *The Hamlet*, that whole trilogy, *The Hamlet*,
*The Town*, and *The Mansion*. I found them hysterically funny, and I
remember finally understanding Benjy in *The Sound and the Fury*.
And Walker told me to read the one that has the palms in it, set in
the Gulf Coast. What was it?

*"Wild Palms"?*

Yes, that was it. Walker loved that one. I can't remember exactly what
he said about it when he told me I should read it. Did that one have
a hurricane in it? Well, I remember Walker writing about the hurricane phenomenon himself. I think this whole city understands

the transforming nature of that. It's like the "ex-suicide" he wrote about in *Lost in the Cosmos*. A hurricane has the same power to make big things little, little things become big. The world is just transformed.

*He writes in that passage about how a married couple who come together in the eye of the hurricane and make love, then speak as they haven't spoken together for years.*

Yes, and how everybody becomes so friendly and human and themselves, and normal worries fall off, only to be glommed back on when the hurricane passes and you go back to a Wednesday afternoon. That's all I can ever think of, is how we act when there are disasters. Why can't we just be like that? Why can't we summon that and pretend that there's a hurricane coming so I will be nice to everybody today and they will be nice and we're all in it together? I think that anybody who's ever read Walker will never forget that. It applies so well to life, day to day, same as the Wednesday afternoon malaise. Drive through a suburb—it doesn't have to be a Wednesday afternoon, just drive through one anytime. Here are these dead-looking houses with emotionally and mentally and maybe spiritually dead people inside. That's my understanding of the malaise.

*Like the man in "The Last Gentleman" who Sutter was called to help, the man who had just come downstairs with his briefcase and was standing there screaming with his mouth in a perfect "O." Sutter's treatment for that was to put the man in the terminal ward of a hospital, and two weeks later he was cured. Then the wife took him to a Freudian analyst and he went crazy again, and they sued Sutter.*

Yes, I'd forgotten that, that's great—the man was injected into the eye of the hurricane for his cure. That's hilarious.

I remember that Walker would also talk about synchronicity in Jung. I remember how around our lunch group once how he got a kick out of talking about that and how things can happen like in *The Last Gentleman*, how you can be sitting on a sidewalk in New York and somebody walks by from your hometown. I forgot exactly what he said, but he was making a lot about the sort of coincidences that occur and suggesting that nothing is really a coincidence.

What angles do you intend to take with these interviews? Will it be a book?

*Either a few long articles or hopefully a small book. The idea was simply to gather an oral history, a collection of stories and anecdotes about Percy, and just see what sort of picture emerged. The biographies that were done were all very interesting, but it seemed that they were leaving something out, that they either tried too hard to prove a thesis or that they accounted for all the details with none of the stories or feelings behind the details.*

*I like the approach of gathering a lot of anecdotes from several perspectives to see just how it was that Percy tried to "insert" himself into everyday life. The information that's been shared has had a lot of emphasis on how Percy operated as a citizen of Covington as well. I don't think you can separate the two, the citizenship or the attempts at leading a more ordinary life. I've heard details about how Percy had his routines, and you have to wonder how planned all of his moves were. You can almost see him sitting down to manufacture a list, like one of his characters, of "How to Succeed: Move to Covington. Start a literary discussion group. Write daily. Go to the post office daily. Take dog. Get involved in civil rights. Become a better Catholic."*

That's true, I think. He made a point of gathering everyday people around him. That was part of what he said about our lunch group, that he wasn't out there in the world the same way we were. He said that in gathering us and listening and getting us to talk about things—skiing, a new restaurant, something on the news—that was his way of being in the community without having to use his writing time or his family time.

*Do you recall how things were when you found out he was ill?*

The main thing I remember is that the family had to push people away at the end, and rightly so. The decline was fast. For me, I just wanted to have some final connection or some kind of good-bye. I knew it wasn't going to happen in person, though. He'd already withdrawn from some of the groups, and I think I knew he was very sick before most people did. His time was limited, and he called off our lunch group meetings to spend more time with his wife, his daughters, and his grandchildren. I just remember not knowing what to say and not wanting to say, "Oh, you're going to die, so I need to say how much you meant to me." At some point I sent him something from Europe, a photograph of a solicitor's sign that said, "Percy Walker, Purveyor of Truth," something that the British say about their lawyers. I thought the name was funny because his whole life he'd been called Walter Perry, and Perry Walters, and so forth. It was silly, but it was an excuse to send him something, along with a note to say that I was thinking about him and hoping he was feeling better. I knew he was really sick, though, and I was delighted when I got a card back saying, "This is fabulous, where did you get it?" or something like that. It was like a final connection.

When he died, it was very hard not to get swept away with memories. I think right away it kicked in how lucky I was to have spent as much time as I did with him. I wasn't just a publisher and bookseller to him—he was a sort of mentor for me. I always counted him as really important in my life, and he let me know early on that he was interested in me. That was reassuring; there was a link. He made it so that there was the family link, and the bookstore link, and I felt connected to him. I realized how lucky I had been rather than being utterly devastated. I mean, he had died, so he was up in heaven, looking good.

Given one more call or one more visit, I'd tell him that having known him for so many years and having read his books, that I didn't think it was coincidence that I met him at age seven. I'd want him to know that he'd had a powerful influence on me for the good, to make me a better person, to open up ways of thinking and believing. I didn't realize at the time how big he was in my life, on a genuine level. Part of me before was a little starstruck, or a little father-daughter struck, so I wasn't always taking things as if they were real life. I just wasn't aware of the impact. I was trying to be genuine, but part of me had to struggle to be genuine because I was aware that I was getting something out of it, the cachet of being his friend and his bookseller. It was a struggle to not be false at times. He had to set boundaries for a lot of people to keep from being used, so I made it a task that I would get to know him well enough that he'd never have to do that with me. I think for the most part that worked out.

I do miss him, but I feel really rich in his memory. He gave me a lot, and he propped me up. One of my favorite times was when I was really low and I was talking to him about a potential boyfriend and how I was really mixed up and didn't know if he was going to call me and I was just torn up because he hadn't. Walker said, "Well, it sounds to me like he's got shit for brains, Blondie, so don't even worry about it." It just made me feel so good, hearing Walker say that there was nothing wrong with me, and using this fifties frat-boy way of talking that I'd never heard him use. He just really saw what I needed and he said it. I think you'll hear that from a bunch of people, that he made people feel special.

# LeRoy Percy, Brother

GREENVILLE, MISSISSIPPI

---

*LeRoy Percy was the second of the three Percy brothers, Walker being the oldest and Phin the youngest. As a young man, LeRoy returned from service in World War II to the family plantation in Washington County, Mississippi, near Greenville, to marry Sarah, his girlfriend since high school. After sixty-one years of marriage, Sarah died, not long after this conversation took place, leaving LeRoy grief-stricken. LeRoy died in 2003. Their absences are felt keenly by their families, friends, and community.*

*LeRoy was a strong, confident man with an air of business and an obvious knack for cutting through b.s. He was also a stimulating conversationalist and gave you the sense that anything he said should be listened to, remembered, and acted on immediately, as if an order had been given from the highest command. Perhaps it was this demeanor that led Uncle Will to turn over to LeRoy the family plantation, where he grew cotton, soybeans, and rice. He thus took his place in the long line of Percys who were a major influence in the state of Mississippi. He served on a number of prominent boards; was president of the Greenville Compress Company, a leading ginning operation for Delta cotton; and ran the Trail Lake farms and other Percy properties. His sons and grandsons are now part of the business, which is a major farming operation in the Mississippi Delta region. He spoke to me of his brother Walker from his office at Greenville Compress.*

Well, first I should explain about Walker's being a doctor. Uncle Will Percy raised us, ya'll know about that, the three of us boys. He decided that he had to make preparations for the three of us, and he decided that Walker was going to medical school. First Walker went to the University of North Carolina, just like I did, and Shelby [Foote] went there too.

Then Uncle Will had arranged for him to go to New York and go through med school. He disliked it intensely. He didn't want to be a doctor. The only part of the medical school that he liked was the psychiatric part. In fact, he was seeing a psychiatrist on a regular basis, I think the whole time he was up there. It was a woman, I can't remember her name. [Percy was seeing the psychiatrist Janet Rioch, a protégée of Harry Stack Sullivan.] But the medicine bored him to death, and when he was first practicing medicine is what gave him TB. He ended up at [a tuberculosis sanitorium at] Saranac Lake for a couple of years. Then he came back to New York to try to start back to medicine and that didn't work out.

*Did your Uncle Will decide what you and Phin would do too?*

Yeah, Phin went to the navy and hated every minute of it.

*And you?*

Well, I'll tell you what he did. I started dating a girl when we were both thirteen. When I got to be about fourteen or fifteen, I was way more interested in dating that girl, Sarah, who would later become my wife. We've been married for over sixty-one years. And Uncle Will decided that I was dogging it because my grades in high school weren't too good, you know. So he called Episcopal High School in the middle of the year, in January, and asked if there was a vacancy. They said yeah, they had a guy that just got sick and left, so send him on. So I appeared at Episcopal High School, a prep school in Alexandria, Virginia, in the middle of the year during lunchtime, and I walked into the lunchroom, and all this hubbub was going on, and the minute I walked in it got quiet. You could hear a pin drop—there was a new boy. And they looked at me, and they shook their heads, and said, "My God, Mississippi." So I stayed up there a year, and then I went on to North Carolina where Walker was. He was a year ahead of me.

*What did you study at Chapel Hill?*

Almost nothing. I was dogging it still.

*So Uncle Will was right about you.*

He sure was. I got a B.A. in economics, and I finally got interested and applied to Harvard Business School. And I got accepted. Just when I was getting ready to graduate, Uncle Will got real sick, and he died January of 1942. I had to come home and handle the estate, the farm, the whole business. So I missed out on Harvard.

*You were pretty young for that much responsibility, weren't you?*

Yeah, that's true, but Uncle Will said to me one time, "You know what the average age of an officer in the military is? Twenty-five." What he was trying to say is if you ain't got sense enough at twenty-five, you ain't gonna ever have any sense. He was about right, about right.

So Uncle Will died, and I took over, and that was in the days when we still had tenants, sharecroppers, which was still a form of slavery, really. We had 142 families on it. The farm then was about 5,000 acres. It was nice insofar as the tenants had cows and pigs and their own gardens, except that they were just tenants. The way the thing worked, sometimes a tenant wanted to move. So when a fellow came up and said he wanted to move to a new landowner, that landowner would ask what he owed. It might be up to $400, but the landowner would pay the money, and the debt would follow that tenant farmer, wherever he went. It was a bad system, really. It was one step away from slavery. That system lasted through the war and ended sometime after the war. Today we farm the same amount of land, more really, and we've got only 6 people on the payroll instead of 142 families. That's good news and bad news. The good news is that it's cheaper for us; the bad news is what happened to those 142 families. Most of them just had to go west, migrating and looking for work. There weren't any jobs.

But anyway, the war came along, and Uncle Will died, and I was busy getting all that stuff taken care of, and it took a while. Then I volunteered as a private in the air force, which was crazy. I could've been one of those ninety-day wonders, they called them, and gone to officer school to come out a second lieutenant. But dumb me, I became a private. Boy, I stayed a private a while. Finally, I got to be a cadet and got into flight training, graduated an officer. They kept me there at the airfield to instruct. I was an instrument instructor.

Time moved on, and I volunteered to go into a B-26 group, a bomber. They had a lot of trouble with them. They used to train on them down in Tampa, and they'd lose an engine on takeoff. They used to say, "One a day in Tampa Bay." They called that plane the Baltimore Whore because the wings were short, it had no visible means of support. So I got into that plane, trained, got my crew, and flew a while and got to where I could halfway fly the damned thing. Anyway, I went overseas and the war was just about over when I got there. I got there in February, and the war was over in Europe after I had only been there three months. I flew twenty missions over there. Then they had a system when the war was over in Europe that you'd earn a certain number of points according to the number of missions you'd flown, and you earned enough points, you could go home. I was supposed to complete forty-five, so I asked if I could go to China, Burma, or India. I got a new airplane, an A-26, much better than the B.

Just when I got over there, they dropped the bomb on Hiroshima and the war was over. But by then, I was separated from my other outfit because I had volunteered, so I was unattached. All the squadrons and groups went home, but I wasn't with them. So after the war was over in Japan, I spent six months going from one airport to another in Europe, trying to get home. You ain't supposed to be unattached, and they didn't have a good way to get me home.

I spent most of my time playing poker and was a pretty fair poker player. One day I was playing poker and a guy was standing back there watching, and he said, "The way you talk, you sound like you're from Mississippi," and I said I was, and he said, "Well, I married a girl from there." I asked him whereabouts, and he said from Leland, which is just right over from Greenville. So he says, "I'm in charge of 400 black troops, and I've got to get them all to a Liberty ship and take them home. You want to go?" So I said hell yeah, and so this fellow, Tom, bless his heart, took me on his boat. We got to Boston, and Tom, he was a major, and he said, "Now Percy, I've got to appoint somebody to be in charge of these troops. You're in charge, and you've got to get them to Hattiesburg, Mississippi." I said, "No, Tom, you ain't putting me on that," and he said, "That's it." So he leaves and here I am with this bunch of guys instead of going home.

*You got attached then, didn't you?*

I tell you, you talk about attached. So we took a train, and it seemed like it stopped every hour or so and it took us three or four days to get to Hattiesburg. And whenever it stopped, all these guys would get off, go get beer and cigarettes and stuff. And I'm in charge, and when I get there, I've got to have the 320 troops I left with. Man, I liked to have had a breakdown. I was out hustling them every time, telling them to hurry and get back on the train. So we got to Camp Shelby in Hattiesburg around Christmastime, and I came home, and everything had kind of gone to hell. I had to go about rearranging our farm operation. So that's about it for me, I reckon.

I don't do it now. My son has done it for about twenty-five years, and I have two grandsons that farm. It's real funny—one of them is an M.B.A., and one of them has a law degree hanging on the wall, and now they're driving pickup trucks, and their main job is bringing in flat tires and getting them fixed and taking them back. But they love it, they love it. What they love is, farming is one of the few professions where you don't have to kowtow to somebody. If you're selling, you've got to be nice to the guy you're selling to. If you're buying, you've got to be nice to the guy you're buying from. But if you're farming, insofar as other folks are concerned, you can tell them all to go to hell. You don't have to fool with anybody, and you come up with the same crop. So that appeals to them, and they are the fifth generation of my family to farm out there.

*What was going on with Walker during the war? Did he consider coming back to farm when Uncle Will died?*

Well, during the war he was sick with TB.

*Did he tell you that he had any regrets about not being in the war like you and Phin?*

Yes, he did. Phin, the youngest of the three, was a war hero. He was a captain on PT boats with Jack Kennedy. He was on his own boat with Kennedy the night Kennedy's boat got cut in half by a Japanese destroyer, when Kennedy and his men wound up having to be rescued from the Solomon Islands. He and Kennedy became friends. Kennedy's nickname over there was "Shafty," and I asked Phin why. He said that Kennedy was always complaining that they were getting shafted—they wouldn't send them any beer, and there weren't enough Red Cross nurses to go around. He was always saying how they were shafting the living hell out of the PT men.

Phin got decorated, by the way, while on the PT boats. Then they brought him home to instruct. Well, he went to Connecticut, volunteered for submarines, and got in a submarine and went back to the Sea of Japan and damned near got sunk by a depth charge. Now you talk about a guy fighting the war. He got decorated again. He didn't say too much about it though.

*Good Lord. And so did Walker feel left out?*

He was sick, but he wanted to go. He really wanted to go.

*Based on how he felt about military school, do you think he would've enjoyed the military?*

I don't think he would have at all. Somebody's always telling you what to do. Very few people enjoyed the military.

*Do you think he was being idealistic?*

Yeah. See, our father was in the First World War, and Uncle Will had been in it too. My father never was in combat, but Uncle Will was a real hero. You've read his book, *Lanterns on the Levee?*

*Yes.*

He got decorated over there, Uncle Will. But you know, Walker had been in Germany before the war, and he liked Germany. He went on a walking trip over there.

*I read that he left his group and struck out on his own to see the country when he was over there.*

That's right, he went walking through the Black Forest. He was amazed at what happened over there. He was over there before Hitler. Hell, I was over there with my wife in 1938. We went to Europe and got a car, and we saw Hitler and we saw Mussolini and we didn't think anything about it. We were just busy thinking about what beer we were going to drink. It was crazy what happened. It was funny—we spent three nights at Heidelberg and it was beautiful. We just stayed there and looked around town. Then the fifth and sixth missions that I flew were to bomb Heidelberg.

*Wow.*

I hated to pull that bomb array. We liked to blew it off the map.

*Were you able to keep in touch with Sarah while you were gone to school and then gone to war?*

Yeah, she was my gal. We courted the whole time. I didn't have to come beat anybody else out. That's why I got sent off to school, because I was more interested in her than I was in going to school.

But Walker, he felt bad because he felt left out of the war. During that time that he felt left out was when he wrote *The Gramercy Winner,* and then I think he started on *The Moviegoer* right after that.

*By the time he published "The Moviegoer," Walker was in his early to mid-forties, I believe. What was he doing during the gap between medical school and that time? Did he intend to be a novelist then, or was he still casting about?*

No, he just knew that he didn't want to be a doctor. He made a trip
out West with Shelby and rode horses, and Walker stayed out there
a while. Shelby had to come home for some reason. At that time
we were living in the big Percy house, Uncle Will's house. It's since
been torn down. In the back was a garage and servant's quarters,
a little apartment. Shelby and Walker lived in that apartment for
a while, and their main job was making little miniature airplanes.
They'd spend hours with balsa wood and model glue making those
planes and trying to get them to fly, and every one of them crashed.
Also they made a kayak which immediately sank. It was a disaster.

One summer Walker helped at the hospital as kind of an intern,
and Bunt, his wife to be, was a nurse there. That's how they met and
finally got married. Then they went to New Orleans for a while and
then to Covington. He came up one weekend and they were married and they didn't have anybody there for it—Shelby was there—
Shelby was the only one at his wedding.

*Why didn't he want to have a family wedding?*

I don't know. Just didn't want to go through it, I guess. You know, he
wasn't too much for that kind of ceremony.

Walker was funny. He'd have the television on all the time, while
he was writing, piddling, whatever. I asked him why he always had
that television on, and he said, "Hell, the world may come to an
end." And he wanted to know if it did.

He wasn't well when they were first in Covington. The TB would
come back, and then he'd get better for a while, but he was not
strong physically. He walked a good bit.

*So did he ever overcome the effects of his illness?*

Yeah, I think he had a remission of the TB. He died of prostate cancer. Walker was always skinny.

He took to bird-watching, and boy he was good at it. He had a
bird-feeding platform on the outside of his house in Covington,
and it led to the inside. He had birds who would be eating on the
outside that would come into the house. He got so good that he
could identify the birds by their sound without seeing them.

*So during the period before he got married, what did you think he was
going to do with his life?*

I had no idea. And I had no idea that he knew. He just cast about from one thing to another. What had happened was that when Uncle Will died, he sold part of the plantation and he left the notes for Walker and Phin. He didn't leave one to me because I wanted to keep part of the plantation. And the notes on the plantation weren't due for fifteen years, so he had an income from 1942 to 1957. Of course, after *The Moviegoer*, he did well with his books.

*Were you surprised when the novel came out and got as big as it did?*

It just absolutely floored me. He sent us one of the first copies and I read it, and of course I loved it, but I thought it was so offbeat that it wouldn't catch on. Then when he won the National Book Award, I think it surprised him even more than it did anybody. Then right after that, his second book, *The Last Gentleman*, got put up for that same award, and the book that won it was a book that Walker helped discover.

*"Confederacy of Dunces"?*

Yeah, that won it. And Walker just said, "What a fool I am!"

But Walker, he was funny. Like I said, I think he was amazed at his success. When Walker gave the Jefferson Lecture, he was sick with his prostate cancer then, and he almost didn't go. In fact, I told him not to. But he went anyway. He was not a good speaker, he was not wholly expressive. But it made a pretty big hit, and it was a packed house. I'll never forget, there were a lot of folks there, a lot of folks connected with the government. Then they had a reception across the street, with booze and food and everything, and that went on a while, and Walker was not feeling too well then. That was just months before he died.

What happened was, he had his prostate operation and while he was on the operating table after the surgery, and he damned near bled to death. Came within an inch of dying from lost blood. They had to give him a transfusion. And finally he came home, and we were there, Sarah and I, and Shelby was there, and we were down there from the time he had the operation until the time he died, which was not very long, just two or three weeks.

He would've got a kick out of us after the funeral. He liked wakes.

*Wakes? As in a funeral wake?*

Yeah, wakes. He liked them. So after the funeral, we had the damnedest party you ever saw. I think they went through two or three cases each of whiskey, wine, lots of beer. Priests and everybody got looped.

Of course, you know he had joined the Catholic church.

*There had been Catholics in your family before, hadn't there?*

Uncle Will was Catholic. He left the church, but he was Catholic, and Uncle Will's father was Catholic. Have you seen the statue Uncle Will put over his father's grave?

*Yes, that's really something.*

He worshipped his father. His father was, to him, everything a man ought to be. He felt insignificant compared to his father. Shelby wrote somewhere that he was twice the man his father was, Will Percy was. Shelby was right.

*I have to know a little more about what you said: Walker liked wakes?*

Yeah, he thought there wasn't any use in moping around over somebody. The guy's gone, the person's gone—let's celebrate!

*How did you come to know that he enjoyed wakes that way?*

We'd been to a wake or two. He would have approved of us, he'd certainly have approved.

*Was it that way during your Uncle Will's wake?*

There was no wake for him. That was very weird. He died at the hospital here in Greenville. He had a stroke. He was only fifty-seven. And we brought the casket home to the house, and here I am, Walker wasn't there and Phin wasn't there, and it was up to me to plan the funeral. So I couldn't decide what church. He'd quit the Catholic church. So what I decided was that we'd have a private ceremony at home for just the family, in the house he'd grown up in. But we had to have some kind of priest, so I asked the father if he would come. He came, and it was a cold day. He had an overcoat on, and he never took it off. He mumbled a few words, got his hat, and left. What I think he was doing, was he thought he was breaking the rules. He was put in the position of trying to treat Uncle Will as a Catholic, which he really wasn't.

*With this in mind, how did you react to Walker and Bunt converting to Catholicism? One day he announced that he was married, and shortly after he announced that he had joined the Catholic church.*

I had no idea why Walker became a Catholic. He had never discussed it with me, and it came as quite a surprise. Bunt was raised as a

Baptist. You know, Walker had been kind of agnostic, searching around like most of us do and not knowing what the hell was going on, and all of a sudden he'd become a Catholic. It was a bit unusual.

*It seems that he became pretty steadfast and committed, by many accounts. Do you think so?*

Oh Lord, yes. Walker used to love to take a drink in the middle of the day, which is a terrible time to drink. Well, he'd take a couple of drinks around lunch and then take a nap. I remember one time that Mary Pratt got to fussing at him. She said, "Daddy, if you don't do so-and-so, I'm going to hide the bottle and you cannot have any more drinks." He said, "God, it ain't that serious, is it?" And he wouldn't drink at night, you know. Most people drink at night—that's when I drink.

*Would you tell us a bit more about what Phin did after the war?*

Well, let's see. Phin got out of the navy a hero. This is an aside, but after the war, Phin went to the University of Virginia Law School for some reason, and he was there when Bobby Kennedy got his degree. Why Phin was there I don't know. And Jack, the president, was there. And he came walking down the aisle after the ceremony, and Jack said, "Percy, is that you? My God, what are you doing here?" And Phin said that he was down in Mississippi and was going to practice law. Kennedy told him, "Why don't you get into politics? You'd love it! There ain't nothing like it!"

So as time moves on, Kennedy was going to make a speech in New Orleans and he called Phin, said he wanted Phin to introduce him. Phin said, "Jack, I love you but I can't because I'm head of the Republican Party down here."

*How did President Kennedy take that?*

Aw, he laughed about it. I think he and Phin had been through a lot and were good friends. But Phin, if he'd wanted to, could've been a federal judge and probably been on the Supreme Court if he wanted to. But he's alive and well, and he's retired as a law professor at Tulane Law School, and he has kids. Life goes on, you know. It's real funny. I asked Phin how in the hell he lived down there now, and he said, "You can't believe this, but my retirement pays exactly what my pay was." I said, "Well how long will that last you?" And he said, "Until I'm dead, dead, dead."

*You said earlier that you thought "The Moviegoer" was a little offbeat when you read it, and you didn't know how it would be taken. What did you think about your brother's books? He was very caught up in philosophy and had a pretty comic take on it. What do you make of that?*

Well, everything that Walker wrote about—not everything, but most everything—can be summed up in one word: the search. He was always looking for what the hell the story was.

*Was that just Walker's way of thinking?*

No, I think it affects everybody. Who the hell knows what the deal is? Do you?

*Certainly don't.*

Well, one thing you'll do is, you'll search and try to find out, right? Hell, I think that's what was the underlying theme of his books.

*Do you think he ever reached a peaceful resolution for his search?*

I don't know. It may be that the church taught him, I just don't know. I can't answer that.

*What about you?*

Walker used to say, "Roy, you're a real dog. You're like the guy who sits in a rocking chair on the front porch of a church. You're scared to go in, but you don't want to be too far away, just in case."

Let me show you a picture. My mother was a Phinizy, that's where Phin got his name, which is an old family in Georgia. There were five daughters, and all of them were married at home. Here they are in Athens, a long time ago. My mother was the second oldest.

*Do you remember much about living in Birmingham?*

Yeah, I remember our house in Birmingham well. It was great. I had a lot of friends, and our house was kind of built on a shelf, and in back were some woods. We made caves and had mud fights. When Daddy died, we went to Athens and lived for a year.

*Why were you there so briefly?*

Well, what happened was that Uncle Will showed up. He came to Athens to see us. He came to check on us. He and my father were very good friends, first cousins. We were fascinated with him. He was a charmer. He was one of the most unusual people I ever met. He stayed a night, and then he said, "Mattie Sue, why don't you get in your car and bring your boys to Greenville to come see me?"

And sure enough we did. We drove down there and stayed in the big house and did all the things kids do. I was about twelve or thirteen, Walker was maybe fifteen. Then mother had a tragic accident with her car going into the creek out here. It drowned her and almost drowned Phin. He was in the car. He got out. So that's the history of us getting to Greenville. Uncle Will after that happened said, "Ya'll have a choice. You can go back to live with your grandmother, or you can stay here. Take your time and talk about it." It didn't take long for us to say we wanted to stay here.

*How did you mother's family feel about you staying in Greenville?*

I think fine. They thought we'd be happy here. Poor Uncle Will, here he was a bachelor, a poet, and he loved to travel, and all of a sudden he had three kids to fool with. You talk about trouble—we wrecked his house. And Shelby, he just lived with us. He stayed at our house more than he stayed at his. Uncle Will was an amazing person. If you've read Walker's introduction to *Lanterns on the Levee*, you know how he felt.

*I know that had to be a very tough time for you boys. How do you see the effects of that period on your lives?*

It was tough. I don't know, you can either go under or you can survive. We did the best we could. I think it affected Phin more because he was younger. Uncle Will would stay up at night talking to him. Phin couldn't sleep for a long time. Uncle Will would stay up with Phin, talking with him. That really meant a lot to Phin.

*Do you think those events were the basis for Walker's search, the upheaval in your lives?*

I don't know, I can't answer that. I don't know what attracted Walker to his search. You know, I love that story Walker wrote, with the guy playing golf up in the mountains of North Carolina. He looks up and sees that big cloud and kind of wonders what's going on. I love that.

# Shelby Foote, Author and Lifelong Friend

MEMPHIS, TENNESSEE

*Before his death in July 2005, Shelby Foote lived in the heart of Memphis. His home was a half a day's drive from his hometown of Greenville, Mississippi, where he, Walker, LeRoy, and Phin Percy spent their youths as close friends. By all accounts Foote was like a brother to the Percy boys. The Percys had come to Greenville not long after their father's tragic death, and almost immediately after their arrival, they lost their mother as well. Foote and Percy would later become not only friends but also colleagues during their careers as authors. He remained close to the Percy family for all of his life.*

*Foote spoke about his relationship with Percy from his study, a dark, wood-paneled room in the back of the house filled with books, pens, paper, and pipes. He was surprisingly short, but he filled the room when he spoke. His eyes had the most penetrating stare I've ever seen, and when he laughed, he laughed like hell.*

Well, Walker and I were each other's best friends for sixty years. That's a long time for anybody, but for two writers to be best friends for sixty years is really crazy.

*Your published correspondence with Walker was really interesting.*

We never had any notion that anybody was going to see that except us. Sometimes in there I sound like I'm his professor or something, but that's because I had four novels published before he ever had one. I was aware of a lot of pitfalls that I was afraid he was going to fall into.

*How did you learn to write? Did you train yourself?*

Yeah. So did every other writer I know. I never knew a good writer who came out of writing school. I've known some pretty good writers who got ruined by writing schools—Bill Styron should never have gone near a writing school. It got him started, but . . .

I think you can really be taught how to write for the *Saturday Evening Post* or something. I think you can be taught how to write popular fiction. But as for real writing, any help is an interference. The way you learn is through making mistakes and finding them yourself, not having somebody else point them out to you. All kinds of things are happening to writers nowadays. They're going to school to learn how to write, they're working off word processors and computers, that it's more important to have an index finger than it is a brain, that kind of thing. Spooks me. If I'd had a computer or a word processor during the twenty years I was writing *The Civil War*—there's a host of stuff in there that I ran across by accident while looking for something else. I didn't want any research assistants for the same reason. Even typing it, that gave me another chance at it, you see. All this stuff that they're doing nowadays, I think it'll produce a different kind of writing, but I can't believe it's going to be as good as the kind that I, that Dickens wrote.

*Your work on the Civil War is really very good.*

I find that the Civil War is a huge drama, like *The Iliad*. It has a beginning, a middle, and an end, many high points, a lot of low points, and marvelous characters, all the way through it. Time-Life is bringing out a fourteen-volume edition of it now. I just finished reading the first two chapters of the fourteenth volume, the finished version, and it just reminds me again that that's the damnedest subject anybody ever had. I mean, it winds up with Lee and Grant at Appomattox, Lincoln assassinated, you know, BOOM! It's got everything a story could possibly have.

*I saw mentioned in Blotner's biography of Robert Penn Warren that when Ken Burns talked with Warren about his Civil War project, Warren said that he needed to speak with you.*

That happened in a sort of sequence. Ken was doing a thing on Huey Long, and of course you go to Warren for that, and when he got through filming Warren for the Long thing, they got to talking and Warren asked him what he was going to do next. Ken said, "I think I'm going to tackle the Civil War." Warren said, "You'd better be careful. That's a big, deep hole, and you can disappear into it," which incidentally is true. So the next day my phone rang and it was Warren, and he said he'd been talking with Ken and told him to get in touch with me. They went down to see Walker too, but he said he didn't know enough about the Civil War to talk about it. And he didn't—he didn't know much about the Civil War.

What I had to do in *The Civil War*, what I'm proudest of I guess, in a certain way, is when people tell me they can't tell which side

I'm on. One historian said that I do a good job of being impartial, but he couldn't help noticing that my heart beat faster when the Confederates were winning.

*Do you wonder what the political fallout would have been like if the South had won?*

God knows, God knows. I do know this: This country has two great sins on its soul. One of them is slavery, and it'll never wash out. The other is emancipation. We told 4 million people, "You are free. Hit the road." I don't expect that we should have had a welfare state in the middle of the nineteenth century, but they should've introduced those people into society some better way than that. The Freedmen's Bureau was a joke, aside from being crooked.

I now realize, looking back, that I grew up with an absolute conviction taught to me that a black man is something between an animal and a man, somewhere in there, and that he had to be handled just right or the animal side of him would come out. This is all foolishness, but it was taught to me in earnest. Not directly— nobody said that to me, but it was there. That, and that they were very fortunate to be here and that a little time in slavery is a small price to pay to not be in Africa and to be in America.

*Several people in Covington talked about Walker's involvement in civil rights work for that area. Were you aware of that at the time?*

Very much so. I was undergoing that in Alabama at about the same time, when George Wallace was governor, and I had the only Johnson sticker in Baldwin County on my car. I never had a sticker on my car before, but I damn sure had one while I was there.

I got into trouble with people. When I got there, a Baptist preacher saw me when I went to the post office for the first time to get a box and get all set up. This man came up to me and said, "I'm minister so-and-so from the Baptist church, and I want to tell you how glad we are that you're moving here. We need all the help we can get to keep the niggers in their place." And I said, "Preacher, you're talking to the wrong man."

It was funny. I'd be in a barbershop or a filling station, and somebody would say something about the Kennedys or something, and I'd tell them, "You don't know what you're talking about. That's not true." They'd wonder who the hell I was, and it would lead to shoving matches. It got so finally they would look around and say, "What the hell is this?" And somebody would say, "It's that damn fool writer," and they never bothered me anymore. They just believed I was crazy.

*Where in Baldwin County were you?*

At Gulf Shores. Baldwin County, I think, is the largest county east of the Mississippi. It's a very strange thing—they grow great vegetables there, but they don't have any fresh vegetables in Baldwin County. They send them all out. It's like trying to buy Scotch or tweed in England.

Now where are you from?

*South Alabama, near Mobile.*

We came close to building a house while we were in Gulf Shores. Went down there and spent six months down there trying to figure out how to build it. Had a real good architect down there, and what we had drawn up was a three-story house with glass all over the place, sliding doors and everything. The top two floors had a nine-foot gallery all the way around, and what we found out when we got down there was that in a sixty-mile-an-hour wind it would fly. So we didn't build it. But it was fun trying to figure out some kind of way to build it.

The damned fool thing, we had 100 yards on the Gulf and 100 yards on the lagoon back there, a wonderful place. We laid the deposit on it, about $10,000, and when we didn't build the house, we let the option go. That piece of property sold about five or six years later for about a million dollars.

*I believe it. In my home county, one of the men who got his family started in the forestry business in the 1920s had an option to buy a large piece of Gulf Shores while he was purchasing timberland in the southern part of the state. He turned it down because the soil was too hard for growing pine trees.*

I like that area, around Mobile, very much. My daddy died in Mobile in 1922. He was fixing to be manager of one of the best companies in the South, and he was thirty-one years old. When he and my mother got married, he had no plans for working at any time in his whole life. His daddy had everything paid down, a big plantation, and he thought he was going to live the life of a titled man, and his daddy pushed it across the poker table. And he'd married my mother and had to make a living somehow, so her father got him a job as a shipping clerk in Greenville, and within six years we lived in Jackson, Vicksburg, somewhere else, and then he was transferred to Mobile to become southern superintendent. To get ready for the job, he had an operation on part of his nose, a deviated septum or something, and he also had a wisdom tooth pulled. And he did not tell the doctor that he'd had the operation on his nose when he had his wisdom tooth pulled, so from the poison of the wisdom tooth, septicemia set in, and he died in about two days. Nowadays he'd be saved in ten minutes from septicemia, but it sure put an end to that.

*I'm sorry to hear about that. It was your Grandfather Foote who lost the farm?*

Yes, it was my father's father who lost the place, Mount Holly. It's on Lake Washington outside of Greenville, and the little town there is called Foote, Mississippi. The house is still there. It was built in about 1855, just before the war. He got it in 1892 or '93. My daddy used to live there, and when I go down there now—it's a bed and breakfast place—I stay in his room.

They did a good job restoring that place, Lake Washington. When I was a boy, it was a beautiful, beautiful place, snowy egrets all over the place, alligators, and everything else. When all the cotton farmers came in, they died, but it's coming back now. There are no egrets there now, and I don't think there are any alligators, but it's coming back. It's a wonderful lake. The man who first saw it, his name was Erwin. This was back in the 1830s. He was an educated person, and he had traveled in Europe and everything, and seeing it in the 1830s he said it was the most beautiful lake he'd ever seen, and he'd seen the lakes of Europe. The house is a sort of Italian villa.

*How can you ever come to understand the loss of the family place that way?*

I wrote my first novel, *Tournament*, based on trying to solve the problem of why a man would do a thing like that.

Now tell me what exactly it is that you are working on again.

*Well, the details of how Walker spent his time have been pretty well documented, I think, and the other books written on him and the Percy family are also very interesting. Those books, though, are more interested in trying to prove a thesis, and the authorized biography is filled with more facts than stories. The purpose of my research is to gather some of the stories and anecdotes and fill in some of the details of Walker's life, to add a little color to the background. Sort of an oral history of what Walker was like, in the words of different people who knew him. It seems that a complement to some of the earlier work might be worth reading.*

*If you wouldn't mind, I'd like to hear your memories of meeting Walker, about your growing up and approaching marriage, your writing careers, and the later periods in your life. I should tell you that I asked LeRoy Percy what you and Walker were doing during the years after college and before your writing careers were established, and he said that you and Walker's primary occupation was building model airplanes that wouldn't fly and a kayak that wouldn't float.*

Ha! Roy always makes everything a disaster. He usually involves himself in a disaster. His stories are all self-deprecating and funny. But yeah, we built model airplanes, we made a kayak. Sold it as soon as we finished building it because the damned thing would turn over as soon as you looked at it. The model airplane was another thing. We made one for Billy, who's now fifty or sixty years old. All Roy's children are about that old now, I guess.

*Do you recall when and how you first met Walker?*

Sure. I was out at the club swimming, and Mr. Will played golf in those days. He was a terrible golfer, but he played. He'd just finished playing a round of golf and he saw me and came over, and he said, "I've got three young cousins coming to spend some time with me, and I'd appreciate it if you'd come over and help entertain them." I said I'd be glad to, and that's how I came to know Walker.

Walker and I were friends from the start. Walker's six months older than me, so I used to kid him all the time about what it was like to be so old. We both were readers, so we could talk about that easily. Funny thing is how three-quarters of our lives together, I was a great champion of Tolstoy, and he was a great champion of Dostoevsky, and I used to infuriate him by saying that Dostoevsky was the greatest slick writer that ever lived. But we were going back across the causeway, this was in the seventies or eighties, and he said, "I want to tell you something. You were right about Dostoevsky." After all that time!

*Now you always wanted to be a writer, didn't you?*

Never thought about anything else.

*But Walker did, didn't he?*

Walker always wrote something or other. He had a column in the high
school paper, he wrote a lot of poetry in high school, it won a prize
too, and he went to field meets in Latin because he was always
interested in Latin, through four years of high school. He kept on
with it through his life too.

One of the reasons *The Last Gentleman* has that title is Walker
had the influence of an enormously attractive book called *The Last
Puritan* by George Santayana. He was crazy about that novel. I kept
after him not to let *The Magic Mountain* get in his way of writing a
real book about the TB sanitorium. I always hesitated to tell anybody what to write or anything else, but he seemed to be made to
write that, and I told him not to let Thomas Merton's book inter-
fere with that. He just wasn't interested in discussing that with me.

There's a whole secret side to Walker that he hid from various
people. From me, he hid two big things. He did not then say that
he'd already written such a novel and it didn't work, which he had.

*"The Charterhouse"?*

Right. I never saw that one. I saw the other one, called *The Gramercy
Winner*. I read *The Gramercy Winner*, and I think it's at Chapel Hill,
in the archives.

*"The Charterhouse" is the book that's lost, right?*

He destroyed *The Charterhouse*. But I never knew that Walker had written such a novel. He never said to me, "That's good advice, but I've
already taken it and it didn't work."

The other thing he never told me was that he'd ever seen, in
any real way, a psychiatrist. He never told me when he was in med
school in New York, at Columbia, that he'd been seeing a psychiatrist, let alone two or three times a week.

*LeRoy said that Walker was never really interested in being a doctor,*
*that he only cared for psychiatry.*

He's not wrong on that because Walker was going to choose between
two fields of medicine: one was pathology, and the other was psychiatry. He was thinking very seriously about being a psychiatrist.
I don't think he wanted to practice regular medicine. It just didn't
appeal to him. He finally reached the point that he didn't want

to have anything to do with medicine, except incidentally, and he found a way to get out of it. He got tuberculosis.

*When did you find out that he had been seeing the psychiatrist?*

Oh God, way up, way up. He told me he'd seen a psychiatrist while he was at Saranac, but they couldn't effect a transference and he just dropped it. He didn't say, "But I did see one at New York."

That secret side of Walker, you were just not aware of it. I was not aware that he was hiding anything from me. I never even suspected because we told each other the truth about everything. He just had a side to him that he kept to himself. It's very much in character, but it was undetectable. He seemed perfectly open.

I don't think, and there's nothing unusual about this, I don't think anybody will ever really get Walker into a biography. Jay Tolson came closest, but even that didn't get it all. There's a funnier side to Walker that never gets into the book. He could be sardonic in all kind of ways, like one time when we were sitting on his porch, and this fella named Charley Something who walked funny, he was messed up and all bent over, came by. Walker looked across and he said, "You know, ain't nothing wrong with Charley. He just doesn't give a damn." He was like that.

*You catch some of that in his novels, like the man in "The Thanatos Syndrome" in the bar who seemed to be listening and agreeing to everything the character said. It turned out that the man was nodding from Parkinson's disease and didn't know or care what he was saying.*

My favorite of Walker's books for all kinds of reasons is *The Last Gentleman*. He took on the main problems of his life and laid them out. I like that better than *The Second Coming*. He said that when he was writing *The Second Coming*, he didn't realize that was Will Barrett until he was halfway through it. Said he had to go back and fix that.

*During that earlier period, after the sanitorium and before he married Bunt, when you lived behind the Percy house and you made the trip out West, did you have any idea what Walker was going to do with his life?*

Even he didn't know what he was going to do with his life. The main thing he was concerned with was getting well. He wanted to do whatever would make him get well, and he thought maybe the answer was the dry air of Arizona or New Mexico. That was one of the reasons he went there. In fact, that's about the only reason he went there. He grew to love it there. Santa Fe haunted him all his life. But that was what he was concerned with. He was reading steadily while he was at Saranac, and he did an awful lot of reading on existentialist philosophy. That hooked him onto Dostoevsky and onto psychiatry in general.

But probably the number one thing that happened that affected his writing and affected his life was Anne being born deaf. That's where his interest in writing really narrowed down to exactly what was going on here. A good example of that is that they discovered, totally by accident, that Anne was deaf before she was a year old, which was rather unusual in those days. Nowadays they test babies as soon as they're born. But it was really not unusual to wait until a child is two or three years old before they found out he was really deaf. Anne was profoundly deaf. Nobody is totally deaf, but she came about as close to it as you can come.

So he was determined to do something about that just as he had been about his tuberculosis. He was prepared to move to St. Louis, where there was a school for the deaf. He went up and looked at the school and didn't much like it. Didn't much like their methods, and he always despised sign language. He didn't want anything to do with signing for the deaf. Anyway, my reaction when he wrote and told me that Anne was deaf—he even told me about how they found it out with the shotgun and the snake and all that. My wife, Gwen, was married then to a leading ear surgeon here named John. John and I were friends—up to a point. Anyway, I went to John and said that a good friend of mine was needing some help, and John comes pretty close to being a genius with the ear. He said there was a woman down in Florida named Mary Lee, and that he thought she was a true genius with the deaf, but she does it on a one-on-one basis. So he gave me her address for Walker to write to her and see if she'd be interested in working with Anne. He and Bunt got in touch with Miss Mary Lee, and she came and lived with them for three or four months. It was she who was responsible for Anne being as functional as she is today. That's one of the reasons Walker got so interested in Helen Keller too.

My reaction, when they told me Anne was deaf, was, "How awful!" My second reaction was, "Well, if I'm going to lose one of my five senses, God knows that's the one I'd rather lose." And man, I was wrong. A deaf person is cut off from the world in many ways far worse than a blind person. You don't understand the rhythms of life. You don't understand language and how it does certain things. And you never really get in touch with life if you are profoundly deaf. Now I don't mean by that to say that a deaf person will never amount to anything, not at all. It's just that if you had to lose one of your senses, believe me, your hearing is not an easy one to lose. It's a tough one, and Walker knew that. That got him profoundly interested in language, in all kinds of ways.

I'll tell you another funny thing about Walker. I had sort of a standard Delta boyhood, meaning I got engaged in probably 32 fistfights and went to 332 dances. Walker didn't like to go dancing, and he'd never been in a fistfight in his life. He never backed down from anything, but there just never was an occasion where he had to fight. He could get awfully angry, but somehow or another he never got mixed up in this foolishness, ducking down in an alley to fight.

*What would set his temper off?*

Well, he could get mad at waiters and parking attendants. I don't know why, that's just Walker. He could get mad at a hotel manager who'd given him a bad room, he'd get really mad about something like that. The other thing too, though, is he was always conscious that he'd never been without money. That bothered him a little bit, and of course he lived during the Depression and he was surrounded by people who didn't have anything. For the rest of his life, he didn't want anybody helping him into a coat, he didn't want servants, and he never liked flashy things.

I persuaded him once to buy a Lincoln from Chink Baldwin down there in Covington. He had it for two years, and he hated that car. It was ostentatious, and he'd rather be in a pickup or something. He was funny about that. He never bought expensive clothes or anything like that. He never wanted any indication that he was well-fixed. I think he was glad enough not to have to scramble for a living, but he never wanted to be ostentatious to any degree whatsoever.

*Interesting. Now in light of what had happened to your family's losing the plantation, did that mean that you were coming from the other side of the economic fence when you became Walker's friend?*

No, it wasn't that way in Greenville in the first place. One of your best friends might be the son of the chief of police, and the other best friend might be the son of the president of the bank. So no, there wasn't that between us. It's hard to say. Greenville was a strange place to grow up. We had more writers per square mile than any other place in the United States. That is not the result of any coterie passing around manuscripts or something. We didn't do that. It was just the example of Will Percy, who had published books and was a cultured man with a sizable library—not that he ever shared it. Mr. Will wouldn't lend anybody a book under any circumstances!

But about that library, I got expelled from school, and Mr. Will went to see my mother and said, "Shelby's in all this trouble, and he doesn't belong at home without anybody in charge. Send him over to the house and let him stay with me." Walker and Roy were both off at school, and Phin was there, and he and Phin had a good time together, so I did. And man, I never did so much reading in my life. I went through the whole Percy library.

Will Percy, though, was an extremely important person in Walker's life. Mr. Will was a great teacher. He could be talking about Keats's poetry, and he would get you so interested in it that you wanted to end the conversation and go read some Keats, which was exactly what he wanted. He could do that better than anyone I know. But he had a huge blind spot. He never could read Proust. He thought John Crowe Ransom was a bad poet. He had all kinds of really debilitating blind spots for some writers.

*So you respected and revered Will Percy as much as Walker and the other boys?*

Very much. Absolutely. People don't know about Mr. Will. He had one of the fiercest tempers of anybody I ever saw. We were scared to death of him, if he got angry. We broke a chandelier. Phin had some tennis balls and he wanted to play tennis, and Mr. Will had a Venetian chandelier that was circular, it had a circular glass trough, and I put Phin's tennis balls up in there. He came looking everywhere for his tennis balls, and he finally happened to look up and see them through the glass. Well, he got on a tall chair and turned the chandelier so the tennis balls would come to where he could reach them, and the whole thing went crashing to the floor. Oh, my God. Walker said, "I didn't have anything to do with it," and LeRoy said, "We've got to accept full responsibility and go tell Uncle Will about it." So we went down to Mr. Will's law office, and we were scared. His mother had gotten that for the house. So we said, "Uncle Will, the chandelier in the library, it got broken." And Uncle Will said, "What do you mean it got broken?" And LeRoy said, "We" — not "Shelby," but "we" — "We put the tennis balls up there and Phin was trying to get them back and the whole thing came crashing to the floor." Mr. Will said, "Goddamn it! People who don't know how to take care of things shouldn't be allowed around them!" And it just flabbergasted us, he just flattened us with those kinds of comments. But he would get over it.

Mr. Will's mechanical aptitude was pretty miserable. The boys got together for Christmas one year, this was in the thirties, and they had bought him a radio with push buttons on it for different stations. And the little push buttons had a little set button under each one and a label under it that you would write the name of the station on. We showed Mr. Will how to work it, how you push the buttons to get the station. We came out the next day and he said, "This damn thing won't work." He had pushed the set buttons and they wouldn't work, and he had broken all of them trying to get it to play. He couldn't begin to operate it.

Mr. Will never knew how to drive a car either, another example of his lack of aptitude for anything mechanical. He had, back in the twenties and early thirties, a town car, where the chauffeur sits out in the rain. It was amazing to everybody in town that there was any such car in Mississippi, let alone right there in their home-town. He didn't have this thing like Walker about flamboyance. He didn't mind at all. He didn't give a damn whether anybody thought he was putting on airs.

*LeRoy said that Uncle Will planned what each of them would do for their education and their careers.*

He was one to do that. I was in a deep discussion with him one time over God knows what, and Mr. Will says, "I know what you should do: you should join the navy." I thought, "Have you lost your mind?

I don't need to join the navy!" I didn't say that to him, though, I just shook my head. But he would do that. He got a friend of ours married so fast, he didn't know what he was doing. This fella had been going with this girl for a long time, and we were up at Sewanee, and he mentioned something about her. He said to Mr. Will that he had half a mind to marry her. Our friend was a bachelor of about thirty-eight by then, and Mr. Will said, "Send her a wire and have her come up." She arrived the next day, and they were married in the chapel in Sewanee, and Bob blew his brains out about five years later.

But Mr. Will, he would tell you what to do in a minute. He would guide people in ways he thought they ought to go. Each of those three boys did what he wanted them to do. I don't mean he ordered them to do it, but he had this idea that LeRoy would run the place, Walker would be a doctor, and Phin would go to the Naval Academy, and by golly, that's what they did.

*What about you? What did he advise you to do, other than the navy?*

He was unsuccessful. He didn't really try to handle me the way he handled the three he was responsible for.

*Did he advise you to go to school at North Carolina?*

No, but he researched the hell out of that school for Walker. He'd reduced the choices of schools to two. One was a school in Florida called Rollins. It was a very interesting, experimental school—they had outdoor classes and all sorts of things going on there. The other was Chapel Hill, which had the best English Department in the South, and of course they still do. But they decided on Chapel Hill, and because Walker had gone to Chapel Hill, I wanted to. I probably wouldn't have gone if Walker hadn't.

*How did Walker feel about Carolina?*

He liked Chapel Hill; he enjoyed it.

*And when you went to Chapel Hill, had you decided how you would use your education to pursue a career in writing?*

What I did was, I turned Chapel Hill into a liberal arts university, kind of like what my son went through. He went to school at my wife's college, Sarah Lawrence, and you could take what you wanted to take. I did that at Chapel Hill—I took what I wanted to take and didn't take anything I didn't want to take. By the time I hit calculus, I knew I was through with mathematics forever. I even sat in on graduate courses, incognito, pretending to be a graduate student. I spent more time in the stacks at the library than I did in class. I just used the school the way I wanted to use it, and it was perfect for that. They had good teachers there.

Walker had a really good German teacher, which resulted in his going over to Germany around 1938. He saw the Nazis in full flower.

*Considering your own career, you were interested in the Civil War, but Walker said that he hated the term "southern writer" for himself.*

He did and he didn't. I used to argue with him, and I'd tell him, "I don't care what you call yourself, you're a southern writer, God-damn it, like Marcel Proust was a Parisian writer." And he admitted that to me. But he also used to say that he never learned anything by listening to old folks talk, and he learned a lot listening to old folks talk.

*He was in such good company to be called a southern writer, though, wasn't he?*

He didn't want to be squinched down in any way.

*Interesting. Now Walker left Greenville, went to Chapel Hill, and then went on to New York. When he came back, rather than going to Georgia, Alabama, or Mississippi, where there were still family ties, he went to Louisiana. Any southerner knows that Louisiana is sort of the South but not quite. It's really a world of its own. Was he avoiding the traditional Deep South, or his family, by going to New Orleans and then to Covington?*

Well, that was because of a sort of accident. Bunt was working in New Orleans, and that's what pulled him there. Besides, people from that whole region were pulled to New Orleans anyhow. It was also the church because he was thinking about conversion. He told me that when we were in Santa Fe, that he was thinking about it seriously, before he was married. Of course, he got married by a Baptist preacher, a man who had hair like a chicken was sitting on his head. I was the best man in his wedding.

*You were the only man, I heard.*

That's right! Anyway, Walker gave me an envelope with a 50 or 100 dollar bill in it to give the preacher after the service, and I didn't know how to give this man money, tipping him or whatever you call it. I didn't know how to do that. So I had it, and I was trying to figure some kind of way to say, "Here you go," or something, and out of nowhere this hand appeared and I just put the money in it. It solved itself. But in the ceremony, Walker had gotten a wedding ring, it was platinum, and I had to have it to hand it over. So the preacher had a little sermon there, advice to the bride and groom, which I am utterly opposed to, but anyway I remember he said, "May the love in your marriage be as pure as the gold in this ring." Then he saw the ring.

*I understand now why he moved to New Orleans. Afterward, though, they settled in Covington. I was wondering if you thought that he resisted coming back too close to places where he had tough memories.*

I think so. But I also think he thought he could have a better life in the vicinity of New Orleans than he could in the vicinity of Memphis or Greenville. It was a natural place to go to. The fact that Bunt was there already helped too since he had to go there from Santa Fe. But when he told me that he was considering conversion to Catholicism, I was horrified, absolutely horrified. I didn't know anything about the Catholic church, just that every now and then they gave you messages on a card, this, that, and the other, but above all, I knew that there was a whole list of books they can't read. I said, "Yours is a mind in full intellectual retreat." Jay Tolson tells about that. He said it was a wonder we ever spoke again.

*Did he get mad at you about saying that?*

He didn't get mad at me, he got mad at the idea. He said, "You just don't understand at all." And of course I didn't. He was right—it was exactly what he needed. It was at the very center of what he was looking for. He got a great deal from the church then, and when he was dying too.

*What exactly did he get from the church? LeRoy said that Walker can only be understood in terms of "the search," and when I asked LeRoy why Walker converted, he said that he had no idea.*

Walker always needed or admired a kind of authority that gave his life a core. The so-called broadsword virtues or southern virtues or Marcus Aurelius and the rest of it—he didn't have much use for that kind of sentiment in life. But he had a certain admiration for something else. At first he had a certain kind of admiration for the Nazis, which is hard to believe, but this was in the early days where the reports were that they were bringing order to what in

Germany had been chaos. And the church was really an answer for him. What's more, he was interested in a very serious way. He truly studied the Bible, which his father had done before him, especially Revelations. He read Aquinas and read all the modern philosophers, like Maritain, to their depths. I always thought that he made other Catholics feel like they were Baptists because he knew the church so well. He was, a couple of years before he died, on the American committee advising the Pope, and he gave advice to the Pope. Protestant evangelism was making such a headway in South America, mainly due to television, and he wanted the Pope to start doing a Mass on television, which hadn't been done. That was one piece of advice he gave.

He didn't like some of John 23rd's reforms. He didn't like that business of shaking hands at the end of the ceremony. He didn't like losing the Latin Mass. He went with it, and he was a great admirer of the present Pope, John Paul, but John 23rd shook it up too much to suit him. Walker wanted to join the old church.

*So in addition to his religious search, you think it was the appeal of the structure and the authority of the church that appealed to him.*

It did, indeed.

*That brings to mind the sort of men who raised him. That may even suggest his response to the loss of his father.*

He could make jokes about it. He would say that the main thing that shows the church knows what it's doing is how it's survived its own membership. But he always called himself a bad Catholic for some reason.

*Did you get a sense from Walker of the kind of fellow his father was?*

I heard some things that were not too good to hear. He would pit those two boys against each other and enjoy watching them have some kind of contest.

*Walker and LeRoy?*

Yeah. LeRoy remembers that too, and he doesn't like it. It was a strange household that way during the last couple of years of his life. He was in great distress about God knows what all. He had made suicide attempts before that, had bandages on his wrist, things like that. I don't know what was the matter with him, I really don't, but he killed himself in the same way as his own father had.

Walker, LeRoy, and Phin have all lived under the shadow of this threat of depression and suicide. This goes back. It's not only his father and grandfather. Poor Thomas J. [Percy] killed himself too, way back.

*Was there an element of manic depression in Walker? A few folks who described Walker said that he often appeared agitated, sometimes worked up about something, fidgeting and scratching, nervous. Is that accurate, or was that sort of behavior rare for Walker?*

There's a lot of truth in that, that somebody would see him that way. I didn't. He didn't seem that way at all to me, but I could see how somebody could think he was, yeah. Another thing to understand about Walker, while we've been talking about so many of his influences, was that in Bunt, Walker found exactly the wife he wanted. He came up here to Memphis one time to the opera, and we were there waiting for it to start, and a party came in and sat a couple of rows in front of us. Walker saw this girl in the group and said, "My God, it only happens once in your life. That is the very person for me." It was a girl who later I got to know well named Liz Farnsworth. And I said, "Jesus, Walker, go tell her so—right now! Get up and go tell her so!" After the opera, there was a dinner party that we went to, and a friend of ours was there and his partner was Liz Farnsworth. Walker found out she'd been to Vassar, and that was the end of that. He didn't want to have anything to do with a Vassar girl.

*Why not?*

Just because she went to Vassar. It's like not liking that Lincoln automobile.

We had a funny experience. I told you earlier that Walker was never in a fistfight. We were at Chapel Hill, and a group of six or seven of us used to get into a car and prowl around and go to a German place that had good beer there, this was around 1937 or so. We'd go in there and drink beer for the weekend. We all went up this one time, and there were these older men up there, about thirty-one or so, with their girls. We started flirting with the women and took up with them some. Those men resented the hell out of it, so they called us outside. We went outside, and this woman was there, and these men were gathering around, and one of them made a move toward Walker and me, and I hit him, to get him off. In those days, you wore a dark coat and light trousers. Well,

Walker and I had on black trousers and a white coat, both wearing the same thing. The woman thought Walker had hit this man. She grabbed Walker by the front of his shirt, pulled him toward her, and punched him. He put that in *The Last Gentleman*. Anyway, another man, built like a bull, came rushing out of nowhere, grabbed Walker, and carried him over backward on the ground and was over him. I came up behind him and grabbed him to pull him off of Walker, and he was so big around in the chest that I couldn't get my hands together around him, but I pulled him off. As he was getting up, I said, "We don't want any trouble." I didn't want any trouble with this man for anything. That's the only time I've ever known Walker to be in a fight. And all he could say was to tell that girl, "You're a woman! You're a woman!"

*Did you settle in Memphis around the same time he settled in New Orleans?*

He was there before I was here. I think he settled there in '47, we were in Santa Fe in '46. I went straight on back home and continued writing. I wrote five novels in five years, then I moved to Memphis in '53. Walker was in New Orleans, and they heard that Covington was especially healthy because of its numerous longleaf pines. It was known as the Ozone Belt. That was very attractive to Walker, who was allergic to everything on earth, including oak pollen. He'd turn purple from that. Now we know that ozone is the deadliest thing in the world, so they don't advertise themselves as the Ozone Belt anymore. The idea was that the longleaf pines put out this healthy sort of thing that they called ozone, but we know now that wasn't the case. But that attracted Walker there, and that was before the causeway was built. You had to drive all the way around through Slidell to get to Covington from New Orleans.

*Regarding Walker and depression, apart from his seeing the psychiatrist while he was in med school, did he suffer from other major bouts of depression?*

I am not aware of Walker having any big problem with depression. For one thing, God knows this has been a savior, but Lincoln concluded that having a real sense of humor is a big help, and Walker had that. He could see the absurdity of things all the time. It helped a lot. He could even see the absurdity of his own depression. Lincoln could really do that. From what I understand, he had a lifelong problem with depression, which he solved. And so did Walker. And so have Roy and Phin.

It was such a horrible thing. His father committed suicide, and then his mother's automobile accident, which Walker was convinced was suicide. Hers was a reaction to her husband's suicide; his was a reaction to depression.

*Do you think he had grounds for believing that his mother's death was a suicide, or do you think he was just reacting that way because of his father's suicide?*

I don't know exactly what Phin told him or didn't tell him about that wreck. There were stories that his mother had tried to take Phin with her, hung onto him after the car was underwater, and he had to break loose and get out. I never believed that. But I'm inclined to think there was a strong possibility that she went off that bridge on purpose, but I have trouble believing that she tried to hold Phin in that car, underwater. Although if she went off that bridge on purpose, she took Phin with her.

So Walker had all that to think about. We talked about suicide a great deal, and we swung all over the place on it. Sometimes I'd think anybody who'd commit suicide would have to be crazy because it's an actual violation of every basic instinct we have. On the other hand, I think it's a very brave act for somebody to end his suffering by blowing his brains out. Walker may have thought so too, but as he said in his last letter to me, in his religion, it wasn't allowed. He said to me, "After going through all this, it's a wonder that more people don't end it. But they don't. My faith won't allow it for me, but I wonder why more people don't do it."

*Is that the sort of comfort that you say Walker got from the church in his last days?*

Walker went all the way. He believed in Jesus Christ, the teachings of Jesus Christ, the future life, hell and heaven, he bought the whole package. None of which I believe. Or ever did.

*In the correspondence, there seemed to be some tension between you two on that subject.*

Right. But we never fell out about things. I said somewhere that we knew what would make each other mad, and we always avoided those subjects, except on purpose.

He was a true friend, though. One time I was mad at LeRoy,

and we were down in Covington. I said, "That shithead," and when Walker got disturbed, he stammered. He said, "You . . . talk about my . . . brother." Then he said, "And what's more, Roy came in here last week and he was running you down, and I ordered him out of the house." It was a wonder he didn't run me out of the house for talking bad about Roy.

*What had Roy done to make you mad?*

I don't know. Nothing, probably.

*Have you ever seen signs of yourself in Walker's novels?*

I've never identified myself as a specific character in Walker's work. I've seen him making fun of me in parts, like the man who lived in a house filled with voluminous rafters. But he used bits and pieces of things, but he never puts an actual person in a place, and neither do any good writers. They put four or five people together; otherwise, the character would be flat.

*I've had a strong impression, especially after reading the biographies, the correspondence, and re-reading "The Last Gentleman," that Sutter very closely resembled you.*

Well, maybe, yeah, some. Sutter is a big mystery. There's a lot of Walker in Sutter, a lot of it. Not only being a doctor, but his interest in viewing sex as a phenomenon. If you take it far enough, it could be a way of life, and so on. Walker and I, we had the normal sex lives of men in our time. We were in and out of whorehouses and everything all the time, in high school and everything. Young girls—unless promiscuity was already established, in which case, anything goes—but a young girl in those days, you would not have sex with her even if she asked you to. You just wouldn't do that. Your girl, the girl you went steady with, certainly wouldn't have sex. There was lots of heavy necking, but no fuckin'.

When Walker called me to tell me that he had cancer, he told me that the doctors had had to emasculate him to cut down on his testosterone. I was astounded. I fell into an absolute silence. I couldn't figure out what to say. I finally said, "Well, Walker, you and I have done enough fuckin' in our lives." He busted out laughing, and I thought he'd never stop.

*You're probably the only person in the world who could've responded properly to him in that situation.*

Another time, while he was very ill, something came out with a photograph of me and I looked like hell. I sent it down to Walker, and I said, "This is what can happen to you if you live too long." And Gwen said, "You should not send that to Walker! You know what kind of shape he's in!" I said, "No, no, he's a black humorist. He'll appreciate it."

Walker called back and asked me about it, and I told him, "Gwen said I shouldn't have sent that, and I said it's alright, you were a black humorist." He said, "Hell, Bunt fell down on the floor laughing, and she's not even a black humorist."

*Knowing that he received a lot of attention for his writing, especially later in his career, I wonder if you think he ever really thought of himself as a good writer. Was he surprised by the attention, or what?*

I think he was absolutely aware of and proud of the attention he received as a writer, and I believe he thought he was a good writer. He knew how serious he was, and he knew he didn't write trash, and he knew that he was onto some things that other writers did not know about. I think he was proud of his work.

*Do you think he knew how well appreciated he was by readers?*

Yeah. People were always after him for interviews, all that kind of thing. I've been going through that for about ten years now. It's a damned burden. You lose your privacy. One terrible thing, which I'm doing now, is you repeat yourself. That's very unpleasant, to be repeating yourself all the time. Some of the stories I've told you were stories I've told others. Some I haven't.

*Does it steal from the time you would write?*

I am not going to finish a novel that I had begun before I started *The Civil War* and took up afterward. I did a novel after that, just to get my hand back in it, but when I went back to the big novel, called *Two Gates of the City*, well, that was thirty years ago. I was a different person then, and I couldn't continue it. I'd have to start all over again, so I didn't want to do that, so I have not gone back to writing novels. I did write some things for the Modern Library about Chekhov which I enjoyed. Incidentally, Walker was a huge admirer of Chekhov. I'm just piddling around mostly, doing what I want to.

*I remember reading your advice to Walker to read Cormac McCarthy, which was before most of us had heard of McCarthy.*

Absolutely. I've been a big fan of McCarthy ever since he wrote *Blood Meridian*. But Walker didn't much like McCarthy.

*Was that because of McCarthy's resemblance to Faulkner, or what?*

I don't think it was that. I think he thought that McCarthy wasn't interested in the things he should be interested in and that he was too interested in things he shouldn't. I liked *Blood Meridian* best, but Walker thought it was a bunch of junk. He didn't say specifically why. Walker had a strange thing about what he was interested in. Walker had an intense intelligence which latched onto ideas, but as for Keats's "Ode to a Grecian Urn," Walker knew it was real good poetry, but he didn't love it the way I do. That was not the way he imagined things. He never really liked Browning, for instance, who is one of the people I like.

*He did like Hopkins, though, didn't he?*

He did like Hopkins, very much. I think that was because of the religion. And I never did like Hopkins.

*For the same reason—because of the religion?*

Right.

*Many people, in speaking about Walker, have ventured opinions about whether he had really found the answers he was looking for by the end of his life. There's a lot of disagreement on that. Some think he was at peace, some think he never found any answers.*

In my opinion, knowing the way he met his death would show me that he got exactly what he wanted from the Catholic church. It was a beautiful way of dying, at home, with his family all around him. He committed suicide in an acceptable way. He did not eat for the last two weeks of his life, he scarcely ate anything at all. The church says that's okay. That's a false suicide, that's acceptable. He didn't want to eat anyhow. At night, when the nurse was leaving, I think his last night and some nights before that, she'd say, "Good night, Doctor, I'm gone pray for you." And Walker would say, "You tell him to let me go. Pray for me to die." He was suffering. But he was amazingly strong. In the last ten days, I would help him turn over in bed. I would hold my hand out over him, and he would use it as a post to turn himself. He was strong, really strong. But there was never anything resembling "Here was the end, right here," staring us in the face, and there wasn't any of our saying what our friendship had meant to us, there wasn't anything like that. Just took it as it came.

I tell you something else about Walker. Walker was forgetting names. He said, "Names? Forget it, they're gone." He had some gaps there toward the end. He and Bunt took a trip to Cuba along with another couple, and he later had no memory of it whatsoever. He denied that he'd done it. I play with the notion, based on absolutely nothing, that his death from cancer saved him from Alzheimer's, but I certainly don't know that. He saw aphasia happen with Mr. Will. That's a strange thing. Ravel died with aphasia—he couldn't play the piano, couldn't write notes down. He appeared perfectly normal, talked perfectly normal, but he couldn't use his brain properly. He had aphasia. I came to Mr. Will's at the time that Ravel was dying. Mr. Will said, "That must be the worst hell on earth, to hear all this beautiful music and not be able to play a note of it or put a note of it down." And here he was, two years or so later, Mr. Will comes down with what he had said was the worst hell of all. It might have been coming to Walker too. You never know—dying could have saved him from it.

I'm developing osteoarthritis. It's terrible. You start carrying a stick, then you carry a walker, then you're in a wheelchair, then they put you in a casket. Terrible stuff. They're no good at treating it, either. They've got some new medicines for it, but they don't work on it. Getting old—I'm eighty-three now. I don't mind being eighty-three, that's fine. But I do mind not being able to jump over that ottoman right there. It's almost impossible. I can't do it. I'd break my neck if I tried.

Now about Walker. Walker was crazy about Mahler, and when he was ill I took him two records of "The Song of the Earth" in translation from the German, and he had not seen the records before. He was amazed at how miserably poor the poetry was. I told him something that I've always believed in—that you can't set great poetry to music, but shabby poetry can make great music. That's the way Mahler's song worked, I think. Of course, the music comes close to making the poetry great.

*You've said that you two have different religious beliefs. What are your beliefs?*

There's a whole side to Walker that I don't know much about. Walker was extraordinarily fond of the whole notion of the Jewish religion. He was a great admirer of the Jews. I had a grandfather who was a Jew. He came over here from Austria when he was seventeen years old, Morris Rosenstock. I think that Walker always blamed me for not following the Jewish religion, since it was there and available to me. He didn't exactly blame me, but he must've wondered why I didn't embrace such a wonderful thing, having a connection to it.

*So how do you describe yourself—agnostic?*

Yeah, sure. It sounds terrible to say so, but art is what I worship, in all its various forms. That's enough for me. That's what I want: art. I don't need any angels playing on harps.

He got way beyond that business of questioning whether there was a God and why we were here. He had no doubt about the existence of God, and he had no doubt that Jesus was his Son. Bodily resurrection. He bought the whole thing. He probably went through a period of doubt about it, but he came back just as strong as he ever was before he died.

We didn't talk much about religion because Walker knew I didn't have any religion and wasn't particularly interested in it. What's more, I found much of what absolutely fascinated him unreadable. I could not read some of that stuff. It just did not make sense to me at all, accepting simple things as if they were profound. Same way with Freud. Freud wrote on symptoms, inhibitions, and anxieties. On the first page it said, "The first thing we need to get clear is that a symptom is not an inhibition." Well, it never occurred to me that a symptom was an inhibition, and here's this big revelation. Hell.

But Walker would know exactly what he was talking about.

*Is it safe to say Will Campbell was a spiritual leader or mentor to Walker?*

Walker liked Will Campbell's down-to-earthness. He liked Will Campbell having Ku Klux Klan members for clients, and he liked Will Campbell being able to talk to people on their Ku Klux Klan level without scorn, although he knew actually how wrong they were. Will Campbell had great sympathy for them as human beings.

*I read Will Campbell's statement that the white redneck was one of the culturally abused classes that nobody ever recognized.*

We were talking about Will Percy earlier. Now years later, I see Mr. Will's book *Lanterns on the Levee* as having one huge flaw. He really disliked poor whites. He had no use whatsoever for a poor white. He was crazy about blacks and so-called aristocrats, which there ain't none, but he didn't like poor whites. Not only Ku Klux Klan members, he just didn't like the poor white attitude. He was wrong about that, just as wrong as he could be.

*Do you think that Faulkner had sympathy for that class of people?*

Faulkner started out trying to make the Snopes the example of every-thing that's bad about poor whites, but he did such a good job that they are not representative of anything, they're just Snopes. The other poor whites in there, Faulkner does a wonderful job with. He's a very moderate kind of fella.

Faulkner once told Ben Wasson, he said, "All these people talk about my having genius. I don't know about that, but I know one time I had genius. It was when I named those people Snopes."

*Didn't you and Walker have a difference of opinion about Faulkner?*

Walker was very aware of something Flannery O'Connor always talked about, the grievous danger of comparing yourself with Faulkner. You could smother your own talent and wind up just like a baby Faulkner. There is some truth in that. There's a real danger of it.

I was with Faulkner one time and we were riding along in a car, and I said, "You know, I have every right to claim to be a better writer than you are because your main influences were Joseph Con-rad and Sherwood Anderson and my main influences were Marcel Proust and you. My writers were better than your writers!"

*Did you ever experiment with the really long tumble of language like Faulkner used?*

Yeah, I did some of that. There was a story in *Carolina* magazine, I guess it was '36 or '37, called "The Crystal Gargoyle." I wrote it right after reading *Absolom, Absolom!*, and it's in the style of *Absolom, Ab-solom!* from start to finish. It's in the library up at Chapel Hill.

I always kept some of what Faulkner taught me in my mind, the way he always kept some of Conrad. The first Faulkner novel I ever read was in 1932, and it was *Light in August*. That's a hell of a first Faulkner novel to read, and it made a terrific impression on me. He was writing about these things right there in Mississippi, where I was. It gave me from the start the idea that in novels you can write about what you live with. You don't have to write about some knight or king or some aviator over in France, some exotic thing. You can write about what is all around you, and you can write about it vigorously. You don't have to be bland just because what's right around you is bland. I won a copy of *David Copperfield* as a Sunday school prize when I was nine, and I had read Tom Swift and Tarzan and all that stuff. And then I read *David Copperfield*. It was a huge revelation to me. I thought, my God, there's a whole world out there waiting for me to live in that's much better than this world that I live in. So I started to read. I didn't turn to serious reading for three or four years, but that's what made me aware of what writing could be and do for me.

*I wonder, out of all the things that have been written about Walker, if you think there is something about Walker that really needs to be said.*

I don't think it's said often enough what a good novelist Walker is. They keep talking about his existentialist views and this, that, and the other, but those books are really good. In the eulogy I gave for Walker at that memorial service, I talked about this man named Carr who said of Dostoevsky that when his psychological wisdom is dismissed as much as his religious convictions are, then we'll finally see what a great novelist he really is. I think there's a lot of that to be said about Walker. Maybe that's why I like *The Last Gentleman* best, because it comes closest to being a great and it has the least of a "message" in it.

There are many sides to Walker. Walker was a great admirer of Mark Twain. Walker was a wonderful writer of dialogue, and he had a good ear for dialogue. He also had a good ear for the absurd mannerisms of speaking that people had, like Mark Twain also had. Walker learned a lot from Twain. He liked him a lot.

*He got "sumbitch" just right and "I been knowing him."*

I've often thought that it's possible that people not familiar with the region that a southern novel covers receive all kind of wonderful surprises, like when Faulkner has that woman say, "I come from Alabama, a fur piece." They think, "Well, that's wonderful," but I've been hearing a "fur piece" all my life.

*Yeah, I been knowing that.*

Yeah!

But all the way through Walker's and my correspondence and friendship, I was constantly saying, "My God, man, don't try to tell anybody anything. You can't do that. A novel's not for carrying a message. If there's one in there somewhere, that's okay, but don't make the message carry the novel." And he was aware of the danger of that because he had messages that he wanted to communicate and he did communicate them, but he learned not to do it in a preachy way. He was a novelist.

# Will Campbell, Bootleg Preacher

*Some people don't have any idea who Will Campbell is. Others have an immediate reaction to the mention of his name, heavy with either admiration or disdain. Will Campbell—he insisted on the telephone that he be called "Will Campbell," not "Dr. Campbell" or "Reverend Campbell"—is best known for his involvement with civil rights and religion. His civil rights work was controversial in just about every way it could be. A native of Mississippi, he lost his job as chaplain at the University of Mississippi ("Ole Miss") for his support of integration. He was hired afterward by the National Council of Churches on Race Relations in the South, which then dismissed him when it found out that he was ministering to known members of the Ku Klux Klan in prison. He insists that poor whites and rednecks have been exploited politically, and he ministers to all classes, all races.*

*Campbell's poor Mississippi background and Yale education have combined to make him the unique creature that he is. He calls himself a "bootleg preacher," and he became a writer on social and spiritual topics, a political advocate for people who live outside the conventions of polite society and the "regular" church. His religious writing led him to establish a working relationship with Walker Percy on the journal* Katalagete. *Campbell became a sort of spiritual adviser to Percy as well—some have even suggested that he served as Percy's confessor. Understandably, he was reluctant to discuss some of his memories of Percy and graciously sidestepped many questions about their conversations.*

*I found Will Campbell to be engaging, extraordinarily intelligent, and lacking in artifice. He is who he is, a man of sound mind and strong principles who wears dungarees and a straw hat. Campbell also has the sense of humor that only a "reformed" Baptist can have. He does his work in a small, primitive log cabin beside his house, and there's a sign on the wall above his desk that says, "No Cussin'," a commandment he promptly and frequently breaks. He repeats his mantra often: "Living for others—that's all that we're supposed to do."*

*Campbell was distracted when I entered his office. Looking for some papers, he told me the reason his office was a mess.*

I have this secretary named Miss Blue, and she hides stuff, you know. I spent a lot of time in the archives down in Mississippi, and I spent a lot of time complaining about Miss Blue. One of the ladies there said, "How long has Miss Blue been with you?" I said, "Seventy-four years. I'm going to fire her or put her in a home or something." Of course, I'm Miss Blue. That lady said, "Well, it's a shame to get rid of her after seventy-four years." The other lady had to come out and explain to her that I was putting her on.

*I just met with Shelby Foote yesterday, over in Memphis.*

Shelby and I were interviewed at the same time once by David Frost or some interviewer. The interviewer wanted Walker, and Walker wouldn't be on it and he told the guy to call me. This was all done in the Superdome in New Orleans, and Dr. J was there, and so was Muhammad Ali. I remember it well because my son was fourteen then and I asked him if he wanted to go. He said no, and I knew he wasn't impressed with Walker Percy or Shelby Foote or Will Campbell, but when I told him who else was going to be there, he said, "Let me get my bags" and came on. We had dinner afterward with Shelby and Walker and their wives. This was during the Vietnam War, and after a couple of toddies, I was really going on about the evils of that war, and Shelby took me on and so did Walker. Walker went to his grave thinking that was maybe not a just war but as necessary as any war we had fought. I never understood that. I didn't already know Shelby at the time, and it got a little heated. Nothing serious, we're friends, of course. You know, a piney woods man—Shelby's not a piney woods man like I am—we circle one another, you know, like two dogs, to see if there's any physical exertion indicated before you go further with this relationship. So that was the circling, and we became buddies after that.

I haven't seen Shelby for a number of years. I remember during the nineties, when I was visiting Ole Miss, that Governor Fordyce had appointed four white males to the Board of Higher Education. That just irritated me. You know, in the sixties with [Governor Ross] Barnett, the Mississippi writers, of whom there are many, said nothing. So I decided that I was going to organize the Mississippi writers, and I went down to Square Books to use their telephone and fax machine and so on. In a couple of hours, I had twenty or twenty-five people who had agreed to sign a statement against Fordyce's actions. I remember somebody asking, "Well, who's going to call Miss Eudora?" Well, nobody wanted to call Miss Eudora, though it turned out she already knew about it by then, but anyway I called her. She said, "Oh honey, you don't have to call me. You know I'll sign anything you old boys will."

Then of course people were wondering about Shelby Foote. Folks were thinking Shelby wasn't going to sign it. He and Walker used to argue about that sort of thing. Shelby would say that the job of a writer is to write, not to be a social activist. And of course Walker did get involved in things like that. So I said I would call him too, and he said, "Sure, I'll sign it, if you think it's meaningful. Put my name on there."

I got to know Shelby pretty well. I worked with Waylon Jennings one summer, after my wife had come to me and indicated that one of us needed to get a real job. I could tell by her tone of voice that she had a preference in the matter over which one of us it was going to be. I'd known Waylon for a long time, and he gave me a job as cook on the tour bus that summer. So we were riding, going to Memphis, and it was right after Ken Burns had done *The Civil War*. Waylon and I were on the bus, and he said, "You know somebody I would love to spend fifteen hours or more, just sitting and listening to him talk? Shelby Foote." I said, "Well, do you want to see him? He's only about forty miles from here." So we called him up, and Shelby always answers his own phone, and I said, "You know, Shelby, I don't know if you like country-and-western music or not, but I'm riding into Memphis with Waylon Jennings, and he would love for you to come over and be his guest for dinner tonight at the Peabody, and if you like, you can go on to the concert on Mud Island with him after that."

Well, Shelby said that he was already supposed to be meeting Waylon in the parking lot on the island at seven o'clock. That was strange because Waylon didn't know anything about it. It turned out that it was Willie Nelson that he had the appointment with. So he said he'd rather meet up with us because he'd never even been to Mud Island before and he could ride with us, so he came and met Waylon and Willie, and then he went on to the concert with us. He liked the music. He was familiar with them—he'd just gotten the names mixed up. And Waylon just wanted to hear Shelby talk. I bet he didn't say 100 words all evening. He'd just ask questions so that he could get Shelby to go on and on.

*Didn't I hear a story about you trying to ask Waylon about whether he believed in God?*

Yeah, that was on that same tour. We were going from Greensboro to Tampa, and Waylon back in those days never slept. He'd go seventy-two hours without putting his head on a pillow. His life was rough back then. Jesse, his wife, was always wanting me to talk with him. She was very religious, raised Pentecostal, and I had trouble doing that. Even when I was an old preacher boy, I thought that was like being a Peeping Tom to go asking people if they are saved and all that. Well, finally one evening we'd played all the gin rummy we could and shot the shit and the other folks were sleeping, and I said, "Waylon, what do you believe?" And he just said, "Yeah." And you know, on a stagecoach bus to Tampa, conversation need not be rushed. So after a minute, I asked him, "Yeah?" And he said, "Ah-hah." That ended my witnessing to Waylon.

But he remembered that, and years later, he wrote a song about that conversation called "In My Own Way." It was on the last album that the Highwaymen did. So we were talking about that years later, and he asked me, "How many books on theology have been written since the time of Christ?" I told him several and that I had one writer friend who put out two or three a week. And he asked, "Well, has anybody ever come up with anything any better than what I said?" And I had to agree that I guess they hadn't. I believe. Help my unbelief. That's what he was talking about.

*Now how did you first come to know Walker?*

I met Walker back in the late fifties. I was down at New Orleans for a student conference at Xavier, a black college. Walker came over to that conference, and he was relatively unknown at the time. I didn't know who he was. We sort of hit it off, and whenever I was in New Orleans, I would go across the causeway and visit him.

*Was this before or after you were at Ole Miss?*

That was after.

*Would you tell us a bit more about your background?*

I had grown up in Amite County, Mississippi, the most rural county in the state. And of course I grew up "Trotting to Training Union," "Every Baptist a Tithing," "Many More in '54," and "Lottie on the Moon by June," all these Baptist slogans. Did you grow up Baptist?

*Family's full of Baptists.*

Yep. Anyway, we didn't have any money. I was just going to be a preacher boy. Nobody around us went to college back then. The few that did went to Southwest Junior College. Back then, New Orleans had the Baptist Bible Institute, which became the Baptist Seminary. You could go into their diploma program right out of junior college, so I decided to try that. Then I preached my first sermon at East Fork, and a fella came by and came over to our house and asked my daddy about me going to Louisiana College. I was very shy back then. I didn't talk. The local people wondered how I was going to be a preacher if I couldn't talk. I told him I didn't know where Louisiana College was, and he arranged for me to see the college the next weekend. I rode the bus there, and he enrolled me right on the spot. Didn't even ask me if I wanted to enroll. Paid my entrance fee. I could barely read and write, but that didn't matter. It was difficult to flunk out of Louisiana College.

*Why was he so insistent on enrolling you?*

He was a strange sort of fella. He and his wife got mixed up in this Anglo-Israel movement, explaining all of history in this cult, and he was really trying to get me involved in that. He paid my expenses while I was there, but then in a year and a half, I left and went in the army and discovered that everybody wasn't the same color and that was alright. Then I came back and transferred to Wake Forest. I went there, then went to Yale and went to school because I liked the pictures I had seen of the campus. I was never a very good student anywhere, though, I don't think.

Then I almost became a Methodist. I just wanted to come back South. I got turned on to race relations, and it was coming on fast and I wanted to get back. I remember there were a number of southern boys there then, including the faculty. There was a joke that New England mothers sent their boys to Yale to get them a southern accent. We had to take a church polity course in our denomination, and I wanted to take the Methodist polity course. The professor was known to be very entertaining, not hard, open-book tests, that sort of thing. The Baptist polity professor was very dry, and I didn't want to sit for a semester under him. So I had to go to the dean and get permission by telling him that they didn't offer my denomination in the course, and he said, "But we teach Baptist polity." I told him that they taught Northern Baptists and that I was Southern Baptist, that they were a totally different denomination. And the dean said, "What's the difference, Mr. Campbell, between Northern Baptists and Southern Baptists?" And I said, "Well, near as I can tell, Dean, it's the difference between a very sick man and a corpse." He didn't press me any more, so I took the Methodist course.

And I got a church appointment to Kenner, Louisiana, and I went to New York, already ordained, to take the discipline exam and be recognized and blessed by the bishop. There were about eleven or twelve of us for the ceremony. We were supposed to march into the sanctuary of this church and sit on the front row, and I was the last one to come in, and they told me when I came in to close the door and get rid of the street noise. Well, I went up and closed the door from the outside, not the inside. Never went in. And I never knew why I did that. But I got on a train and said to myself, "I don't know what the hell I want to do, but I don't want to do this."

Shortly after, I got called by a couple of churches, and I went to another small parish in Louisiana anyway, and then I got into the middle of a paper mill strike and made a speech. The wife of the mill owner, her whole family, were in my parish. I was young and naive, thought I was "the pastor." Turned out she was the pastor and I was a hired hand, and I had to move on.

Then I got a job at Ole Miss for a few years, got in trouble there, worked with the National Council of Churches on Race Relations in the South, got in trouble there too. So I started freelancing and gained all this affluence [gestures to the log walls of the cabin]!

*What happened at Ole Miss?*

It was prior to their integration, but they had a religious-emphasis week then, a whole week of services they had to attend, and it was my job to set this up and invite the speakers. So I maneuvered to invite speakers who I knew would talk on the subject of race relations and the coming integration. I didn't intend it to be the way it turned out, though. We had invited an Episcopal priest from Ohio, Allen Kershaw, and he got on that old show, *The $64,000 Question*, the forerunner of *Who Wants to Be a Millionaire?*, answering questions about jazz. He got up to $32,000 and quit with the money and said he was going to donate it to the NAACP. And sure enough, in the next day's paper, there was a column saying that a priest was going to donate money to the NAACP and that he was invited to speak at the University of Mississippi by the Reverend Will Campbell. That's all we heard for the next six months, discussing this man and the NAACP. I guess with all that exposure, it did lead to some success, but of course it led to my demise. But there were some good people there while I was there. Mostly everybody was scared of all the controversy and didn't know what to do. I didn't take it personally.

*When did you and Percy work on "Katalagete"?*

That was in 1963. Some of my friends had started that.

*After you were fired by the National Council of Churches?*

Yeah. I wasn't fired by the NCC exactly. The Chinese communists used to have a little song, when the communist revolution was moving through, that basically said, "They didn't run us off, they just turned the bees loose in our house and made us want to go." That's what happened to me and several others. But we started the magazine, and Percy was on the board, and he also wrote some good stuff for us.

My favorite book of his is *Love in the Ruins*. That's not his most complex book, and it's not the most recognized by the scholars, I understand. But we were going to put out an apocalyptic issue of the magazine, and he wrote an article for us called "Notes on a Novel about the End of the World," and he got an idea to go ahead and make that novel, and he wrote *Love in the Ruins*. So that's the reason I have a special place in my heart for that book. It's funnier than the others too, I think. Percy always has great humor in his books, but it's a very subtle humor.

He used to read my work, and I would read some of his. Of course, I wouldn't offer one word of criticism on Walker Percy, but he would rip mine apart, which I appreciated. I needed it! But in general, he was always very kind. He was especially kind to *Brother to a Dragonfly*, all the way through.

I wrote another novel that he read and never came around to. It was a satire of what was going on in Southern Baptist circles. He said, "I wouldn't dare try to write a novel about the interworkings of the Catholic church." I told him that I wasn't trying to write about the Catholic church, and I wasn't trying to be a Catholic novelist. But of course he was.

*Did you talk with him about his conversion to Catholicism?*

Oh, yeah, it wasn't anything in any depth, just part of our friendship. Of course, he was married at the First Baptist Church of New Orleans. J. D. Grey performed the ceremony.

*Shelby told us that he wasn't sure how to give the preacher his money, but the preacher just shot a hand out and took it.*

I suspect that's exactly how it happened!

I don't recall that we discussed anything particularly dramatic about his conversion. When I met him, I learned that he was a Catholic. I didn't even know then about his Presbyterian upbringing and his exposure to the Anglican tradition.

*He called himself a "bad Catholic," but Shelby insists that Walker believed everything. What do you make of that?*

Well, I don't want to sound too dramatic, but you're bordering on stuff I don't want to talk about. Some of those things are very personal, and I don't really know why people want to dig into that stuff.

*Could I be so bold as to ask if you served as a confessor to Percy?*

[At this point, Campbell asks me to stop the tape recorder and tells me firmly that he is not willing to pursue this line of questioning. I then turn the tape recorder back on and the conversation resumes.]

*I certainly understand that a line has to be drawn. I find, though, in my reading and in my teaching that people learn a great deal about human nature, and sometimes about themselves, by getting an honest look at someone's life, especially the life of someone like Percy. He couldn't leave personal questions of morality and faith alone in his work, and it's clear that he struggled with a number of serious issues in his life. Lots of people have struggled—I don't think that's a secret. I ask you because there have been people, like Shelby, who've said that Percy bought the whole thing. Others have said that they don't think Percy was ever really a Catholic and that he never found the answers he was looking for.*

I don't believe that. I don't believe it. I think he was very much a
Catholic.

*Shelby thinks that Walker was drawn to you for your "down-to-
earthness" and said that Walker admired the way you could work
with Ku Kluxers and still not approve of what they did.*

I don't know, I never tried to analyze it. We hit it off, and we were pals.
I miss him. But I didn't go to his funeral. When he was dying, I
kept up with him, would call him. My father was dying at the same
time that Walker was, and ironically, he was with my brother, just
a few hundred yards from where Walker lived, right up the river. I
was there at my brother's house in Covington, thinking about how
we were there in Louisiana and two Mississippi men were dying
so close together. One, my father, was a very humble man with no
education, and yet he was very wise. And 200 yards away was a man
of note, literarily and otherwise, and they were both meeting the
Grim Reaper on the same terms.

*So your brother lives in Covington?*

Yes. He went through a divorce there, and it was very hard on him.
He took up with the Church of God, though, and I think it saved
his life. I respected his choice, but I just couldn't get accustomed
to the rhetoric. I felt the same way with Jesse. The rhetoric, it just
bothers me. But it doesn't bother her. And it didn't bother my
brother. Some of that stuff is just crazy. I've seen somebody laying
hands on a commode and praying for God to unstop it.

*I saw that happen with a friend's mom over a broken washing machine
once.*

It's crazy. I've seen folks swear that they prayed a couch through a
doorway when they had trouble fitting it into a room. And they're
always asking you when you're going to receive the Second Bap-
tism of the Holy Spirit. It's bothersome. Anyway, I don't know how
I got off on that.

   Speaking of religion and controversy, though, I remember being with Walker at his house one time, and he had written a letter
about his views on abortion to the editor of the *New York Times*. He
never budged on the question of abortion, and no matter what you
think about it, you have to admit that it's a physically violent act,
on the mother and the child. And he had said in that letter, "We
can't stop you. We're not even going to pretend that we can stop

you. But we are going to tell you what you are doing." Oh, that created a hornets' nest. And I was there, and somebody called him. I didn't know who he was talking to, but at some point, I heard him say, "I will not fight with you. You can go fuck yourself." It was somebody mad at him over that article. If you want to know how Catholic he was, just consider how he felt about that issue.

*How do you get a full understanding of what sort of man he was? Who was he?*

Well, I never gave that sort of thing much thought. I really don't try to figure that sort of thing out. I have no idea who Walker Percy was. Not the slightest idea. He was my pal. What made him tick? I never bothered to ask, and I don't think he would've known if I'd asked. I know quite a bit about him, his life and so forth, but I don't know who he was. He was Walker Percy. That was enough for me to know.

*His friendships seemed to mean a lot to him, didn't they?*

Yeah. But he didn't have many friends. He really didn't have a lot of friends, but those he had, he was very close to. I was one of them, but why, I don't know. He had a built-in shit sensor. I'm not saying that I'm Mr. Authentic Human Being, but I'm not up to anything. I've never been up to anything. I'm not a social activist, really. I wasn't an integrationist either. If I'm up to anything, it's trying to survive as a human being and not a role model. Not going with the flow. Ross Barnett is not going to tell me what to believe, and the Pope is not going to tell me what to believe, and neither is Billy Graham. But I sure would settle for him over the electronic soul-molesters we have today. If there is any such thing as an Anti-Christ, I think the Jerry Falwells, the Pat Robertsons, are going to be it. It's distortion, not only of the Gospel but of their own Baptist heritage, you know. They don't want to talk about the Anabaptists. When they talk about the "old-fashioned Baptists," they're talking about fifty years ago. They won't talk about their real heritage, the ones who wouldn't vote, who wouldn't participate in politics, who wouldn't go to war, vehemently against the death penalty.

*I have to ask you again—and I'm not up to anything: The memories you have of Walker Percy, the things you'd rather not talk about, what will you do with them? Do you intend to set them down in any form?*

No. And that's not to suggest that I'm hiding something or being secretive about Walker Percy. It's just, what would be the point?

Some anecdotes I can share, but I can say that sort of thing about anybody.

We weren't as close as he and Shelby was. But my estimate of Walker Percy, if I had to say—let's just say that Walker Percy was an authentic human being. He did survive. He didn't go with the flow, and he didn't sell out either. He was not up to anything. That's probably why he became a novelist.

*LeRoy said that Walker's life and work were all about "the search." It seems that even when he wrote "The Second Coming," much later in his life and career, his character was still going in search of whether there was a God, setting up the experiment in the cave to prove God's existence. But of course he only got a toothache and had to leave.*

Yeah, yeah. That was good! He got on me about something else I had written in a novel, about a soldier who was out in the woods for three days, and he said, "There's no action. You've got to get in there and try to get the little guy out of that hole of shit or shoot him or something. There's nothing happening there." I said, "Don't give me that. Will Barrett fell down on the golf course and it took forty-five pages for him to get up." He said, "We're not talking about my novel, we're talking about yours!"

*Shelby said that one day we'll get past the religion and the philosophy in Percy's work and realize what a great novelist he was.*

I certainly couldn't say anything about Walker as a novelist. I'm not a literary critic—I just know what I like and what I don't like. I really didn't like *The Moviegoer*, and I'm not sure I even read it all the way through. *The Last Gentleman* I got into more, but it's really his later work, except for *Message in the Bottle*, that I enjoyed.

*Like "The Thanatos Syndrome"?*

Yeah, and the nonfiction piece, *Lost in the Cosmos*. I first got interested in his work before I met him. He had an article in the *Catholic Literary Journal* early on in which he talked about the role of the stoic in the South. Of course, that theme didn't quite go over into his novels and later works. He talked about the stoics, that there was a time when the aristocracy was the best friend that the blacks had, how they furnished the black people with land, rum money, took them to the doctors and so on, but now the stoics are sitting in tight-lipped silence watching the world collapse around them.

They are not the ones providing for the blacks anymore. They're consistently providing only for themselves.

I thought that was a very important insight that he had. Being of the nonaristocracy of the South, of course I approve because I always had a sneaky feeling that my people got sold a bill of goods about the Civil War. That war was a mistake. My grandpa, who fought at Shiloh and deserted and came home and died, he didn't have any business in that war. He didn't have any stake in it at all. He didn't own any slaves, he was a servant himself, an indentured servant. He was not a sharecropper—our people came here as indentured servants. Granted, there was a hole in it. With black slavery, somebody came up with the idea that they didn't have to sell them for five years or for seven years of indentureship, they could just sell them for life.

*I recall reading your ideas that one of the greatest tragedies of the civil rights era was that the white under class never realized how they were being exploited by the white upper class to control the black population. Is that an accurate description?*

Well, I think that the poor whites and the blacks had a great deal in common, and they were both exploited by the white aristocracy. That's an oversimplification of a rather complex thing, perhaps, but the landed gentry of the South, in particular Mississippi, said that we should weep, you know, seeing some of those old plantation homes. My God, the affluence there, that they built on the backs of the black slaves. After the war was over, white people, the poor whites who had for the most part fought the war, were no longer needed by the gentry so they were treated very shabbily. Well, what were the poor whites going to do? They decided they could be proud that they weren't black. I think there was a conscious effort on the part of the gentry to instill that in the poor whites as a means of control. I think it was just that cynical. To me, Robert E. Lee was a very evil man.

*What exactly was the controversy over you having involvement with the Ku Klux Klan?*

Well, I simply got to know a number of them. I helped get some of them out of jail, I buried their mommas and I married their kids, and visited them. I visited Bob Jones when he was in Danbury prison for contempt, and at the same time I visited Dan Berryman in that same prison. I saw absolutely nothing inconsistent in that. There's nothing about ideology in the New Testament or the Old Testament that says otherwise. You are to be with prisoners because they are prisoners, not because of the events, the transgressions. That's never mentioned. I visited this guy down in Angola several times, and he says, "You never asked me what I did." I told him that he was in prison, on Death Row, and that was my interest. Getting him off Death Row.

After the Sam Bowers trial in Mississippi, I went back to try and speak with him. This reporter was right behind me, and he said, "What are you feeling?" I said, "Compassion," and he asked why. I said, "I don't know, I guess it's because I'm some kind of God-damned Christian." He said, "I don't think my paper will let me print that." I didn't much think they would.

A friend of mine from New Orleans after that told me that he was on a committee for his university to choose speakers, and my name came up. I was objected to because I had been seen visiting with Sam Bowers. When he told me this, I said, "So what?" It was guilt by association. I treated Sam Bowers like a human being, thus they didn't want to have anything to do with me. There ain't no easy roads.

*Were you aware of Walker's civil rights work in Covington?*

Not firsthand. I know that helped start some of the federal programs there. As I recall, Shelby didn't agree with that. That's when he was telling Walker that they were writers, not activists. By the time Walker wrote *Love in the Ruins*, though, you could tell he certainly knew the rhetoric.

Walker was a good American. I would go further and say that he was an authentic human being, and he happened to be an American.

# Phin Percy, Brother
NEW ORLEANS, LOUISIANA

---

*Billups Phinizy Percy, "Phin," is the youngest of the Percy brothers. Like LeRoy, he served in the armed forces during World War II; like Walker, he didn't go home to Greenville after the war. Phin served in the navy in two different military specialties, both very dangerous, for a time with then-captain John F. Kennedy, who remained a friend of Phin's during Kennedy's presidency. After the war, Phin came home admittedly restless. He credits his marriage with helping him settle down to work as a lawyer before becoming a professor of law at Tulane University in New Orleans. He now lives along the levee in one of the fine, old parts of town near Tulane in a classic New Orleans home with lamps by the door, an enclosed courtyard, the whole bit.*

*Phin spent all morning with me in his home, sharing family photos and memories about the lives he and his brothers led after losing both of their parents during their childhood. When he spoke of Walker, the admiration in his voice was obvious. It never subsided. He also played a recording of a speech he made in 1991 to the Orleans Club, a venerable ladies' society in New Orleans. I have included a transcription of the speech below because it serves as a nice ending to his recollections.*

*LeRoy speaks boldly in a deep voice that takes over a room. When you hear him talk, it sounds like a good joke is on the way, and then another, and then he surprises you with the depth and clarity of his insight. Phin has a different demeanor, a more rapid, almost excitable voice with a bit of an edge, but mainly he speaks with the cadence of someone who's caught onto an idea he can't wait to share. Painful memories cause him to pause. Just as often as in LeRoy's speech, he surprises you with his wit. Talking with either brother, like speaking with Shelby Foote or Will Campbell, leaves you with the conviction that you've been in the presence of one hell of a man. We began our conversation in a fairly ordinary way.*

Have you been in New Orleans before?
*Yes sir, several times. I really like the Garden District, more so than the Quarter.*

The Quarter was nice when we first moved to New Orleans, but we never go down there anymore. We used to have lunch with Walker and Bunt at Gallatoire's, many, many times, but I can't remember the last time I've been down there now.

*Did Walker favor Gallatoire's when he came into town?*

Yes, he sure did.

*I wanted to ask you something about your time in the war. LeRoy told me that you had come back from PT boat duty and that you went right back into the fighting.*

I was a PT boat captain with JFK in the Solomon Islands. I wrote an article about that called "The Last Time I Saw JFK." But anyway, I came back from PT boat duty and got into submarines. I spent the rest of the war in submarines, until I resigned from the navy.

*Why did you go from one dangerous position to an even more dangerous position, at the height of the war?*

Well, one thing is that I liked combat. Some like it, some don't, I guess, but to me it's the most exciting thing I've ever done. Winston Churchill once said, "It's the most exciting thing in the world to be shot at and missed." I know exactly what he means. The reason I got out of PT boats is that when I got back, after fourteen months out there, I weighed ninety-nine pounds, had all kinds of diseases, but never missed a patrol. So I got back and was assigned to go to PT school up in Rhode Island to be an instructor. I was there about a week, and I went into a drugstore and called a fellow classmate from Annapolis who was in the Bureau of Naval Personnel. I told him I wanted to get out of PT boats and into submarines, and he said okay and he cut my orders that day and I got them the next day. The orders came, I took two weeks off for vacation, went to New York, had fun, then reported to sub school and made three war patrols in the Pacific.

*Did you captain the sub?*

No.

*What was your job on the sub?*

Well, sub school was the best school I've ever been to. I've been to a lot of schools, but when I got through with six weeks of that, I knew what every pipe and every valve was. When I got through, I was assigned to a new sub that had just been built in Portsmouth, New Hampshire. It was called the *Sea Robin*, SS *407*. We went down through the canal, rehearsed a little bit, then went to Pearl Harbor. We made our first patrol in the Philippine Sea, we sank some ships, then the second patrol was in the China Sea. The third patrol was in the Yellow Sea, and we were lucky to get out of there. I started out on first patrol as the communications officer, and during the second and third patrol, I was the engineering and diving officer. I was in charge of keeping the submarine at a specific depth. We sank thirteen ships or so, and to me, danger was just fun. When I was in PT boats, I ran across several people who did not think that. I don't want to say they were cowardly, but I knew one guy who shot himself in the foot so he wouldn't have to go back on patrol. My thought always was that everybody's got to die, what better way to die than fighting for your country? One thing that prompted all this was that I will never forget Pearl Harbor. I was at Annapolis then, and I was so stunned—I still am. How could they do that? That's one of the things that prompted me.

I've often thought that as much as I hated about Hitler, I didn't feel about the Germans as bad as I did about the Japanese. They sneaked up on a Sunday morning, when their ambassador was in Washington talking to our secretary of state. And doing what they did, I will never forgive them. That was what prompted me. I would've done whatever was necessary. When I got to submarines, you got pay and a half because of the danger involved, but I never knew anybody who showed any fear whatsoever. They knew what they were risking, and they did it voluntarily. That's why we only lost 20 percent of our subs—we had 250 during the war, and we lost 50. We almost lost our sub—I guess every sub that went out almost got lost. We had some close ones.

*How long did a patrol on the sub last?*

Usually about seventy-five to ninety days. We had twenty-four torpe-does and were supposed to fire them all. I remember during our second patrol, we fired all twenty-four, went back and loaded up some more, and then went back out and sank some more ships. But the last patrol was the one that I'll never forget. The captain, we called him Stinny, I loved him. I've never loved a person more outside of my family. He died not too long ago. He was the skipper, and we were in the Yellow Sea. That was about the last place you wanted to go—you were surrounded by Japan, Korea, and China, and it was very shallow, and in a submarine, you wanted a lot of depth. It was only about 100 feet deep and very calm, like Lake Pontchartrain. It was not a good place to go. We were in the Yellow Sea, and we picked up an antisubmarine vessel, whose whole job was to destroy submarines.

*Like our destroyers?*

Our destroyers had several functions, but these were designed specifically to take out subs. We knew that if they spotted us on that calm day, we were gone. The captain told me that he wanted 61 feet, 6 inches. It was the first time he'd ever given me inches. We had to have just enough depth for the periscope to be barely above water. We were proceeding toward this vessel to torpedo it, and as we were moving toward it, the captain said, "Down periscope, they're moving." We thought that was the end, that they had spotted us, but we put the periscope back up and they were headed the other way. But as we were coming out of the Yellow Sea around Japan, they had just dropped the bombs on Nagasaki and Hiroshima. We were right over there, but we headed back to Midway, and the war was over.

I don't say this with any pleasure, but I was somewhat sorry. I just loved it. Our next patrol, we had already been told that we were going into the Sea of Japan, between Japan and China. That was very dangerous—once you got in there, there were sitting ducks everywhere. I was disappointed to miss out on that, which was ridiculous. But I was young, and what the hell, it was just fun. This group of people on the submarine were just great. After every patrol, the captain would kick off any officers he wanted to, and the officers could kick off any enlisted men they didn't like, no questions asked. So by then, we had people on there who could do the job. I would've done anything in the world for those people—never asked for anything, never complained, just did their damned job.

*Were you ever depth-charged?*

Oh yeah. We were depth-charged, but the closest we came wasn't actually then. We had some new kind of torpedo we were monkeying around with, and the submarines had been safety-tested to 400 feet deep. We knew there was a 50 percent safety factor, that you could go to 600 feet before it gave way and sank. Well, I was the diving officer and we were going very fast, and somehow I lost control and we went to 575 feet. We sprung some leaks and whatnot, but we got back up, and I apologized to the captain. He said, "Hell, you ought to be proud. Now we know that we can go to 575." That's the way he was.

I had nothing but good times, and when the war was over, I had a lot of great times in Panama, played a lot of golf down there, but it was over, the war was over. I resigned, shook hands, and got on that plane and went back to start a new life.

*Did you think about staying?*

It's like I said in the speech, the game was over. To me, it was like the Super Bowl. You win it, and then you go out to practice the day after? The thrill was gone, the thrill of combat. I got out as a commander. I should've been discharged as a lieutenant commander, but because I was awarded the Bronze Star and the Silver Star, they made me a commander. I had no desire to go through the process to stay in and try to become an admiral. It was not my idea to go to the Naval Academy—it was Uncle Will's idea, and I'm delighted he sent me because I had the thrill of World War II. It was the most exciting time I ever had, and I loved every minute of it.

*When did you decide to pursue law?*

After I had the conversation with Walker about wanting to be a writer and then did some traveling and took some courses, but finally I just decided I'd better do something, and there'd been Percy lawyers for five or six generations. We all knew that Uncle Will did not like the law, and so he never said a good thing about it and had no idea that any of the three of us would get into it. In his plan, Walker was going to be a doctor, LeRoy was going to run the plantation, and I was going to be a naval officer. So I said hell, I might as well try law. I've advised students that it's kind of a no-lose situation, except that it may cost you some money. If you don't like it, you can just get out, leave. But the chances are, if you can just put up with it, go ahead and do it. It's going to help you in whatever you do except being a doctor because they teach you how to think. That's going to help you wherever you go.

When I graduated from law school, even then I didn't give much thought to practice. I did well at Virginia's law school, made the Law Review and Order of the Court, and I could have gotten a well-paid job in New York or whatnot. My classmates were astounded when I applied for the CIA. I really wanted to get back into a war. I wanted to parachute into Russia—I was in the Cold War. I wanted to be a spy, and I was accepted, and I worked in Washington for about six months in the Office of Current Intelligence. Back then, the CIA was still quite small. It had just been formed from the OSS. We worked in a small outfit near the Lincoln Memorial, and our job was for President Eisenhower, in 1952. He had a table of items, and he wanted placed on that table at 7:30 every morning a report from us on everything he needed to know about what was going on in the world. That was our job. I was at the North African desk. I think there were about seven or eight of us who worked there, and I was the only one without a Ph.D. These were some of the smartest people I ever met. We didn't have a clock—we just worked as long as it took. I was beside the Russian desk, and in '53, I remember it like it was yesterday, Stalin died. Of course, Ike wanted to know who would succeed Stalin. They worked all night long and finally finished their report, but I think they were wrong about the successor. But I enjoyed every second of that work.

It took about four months in '52 for the CIA to accept me. They check you out very, very closely. Meanwhile, during that time, I had gone to New York to the World Series and met my wife to be. She came to Washington once while I was there, and because of her, I couldn't be a spy. I was told that I would have to go over and that it would take ten years to build up cover and she couldn't be a part of that. So anyway, I resigned, got engaged, got married, and came to New Orleans.

*Did you apply to teach at Tulane immediately?*

No, we came here, and for a year we just had a good time. We lived up in a place on Exposition Boulevard, which is really just a sidewalk off Audubon Park. We stayed there four or five years, then we began having children—we have four children—and then I entered Tulane Law School because in order to practice law in Louisiana, I either had to take the bar exam or spend a year in a Louisiana law school. I did that for a year, then I left Tulane and became a law clerk for one of the judges on the Supreme Court and then went into practice for two years. I was told by my firm that I did a good job, but I didn't enjoy it. I liked the law, but I didn't enjoy for two years never opening a law book. I was always on the phone, negotiating settlements. I did maritime law, and we represented maritime insurance companies. I resigned from the firm, and it just so happened while going to Tulane that I met the dean, Ray Forrest. After he heard that I had quit practicing law, he called and asked me if I'd be interested in joining the faculty. So I did, and I taught there for twenty-three years. I won't say I loved it, but I certainly liked it better than practicing law. What I found out, and what so few people know, is what a difficult job it is. To me, practicing law was simple compared to teaching. I would get up at 5:00 or 5:30. I didn't want to make a fool of myself, so I would study for two or three hours, have breakfast, go up there, and come back to it. I finally realized that it didn't matter if I made a fool of myself in class, you could have more fun in class. I used the Socratic method altogether, where you have four or five students involved in a discussion about an issue. I found it was the hardest work I had ever done, particularly grading examinations. Good heavens! The things I like most about not teaching are (1) not grading examinations and (2) not wearing that coat and tie every day. It was a very demanding job, but looking back over it, I'm glad I did it.

*It sounds like quite a contrast to being on a submarine at 575 feet. Did the pace of teaching law bother you after all the excitement of the war?*

Yeah, yeah, because the pace was pretty good. I'd always have students who liked to put me in a tough situation in the classroom, asking what I would do if this and what I would do if that. I really enjoyed the class a great deal. I worked harder than the students did, to tell you the truth. You never think about what a teacher does, I know I never did. I never gave one thought in law school to what they had to go through. I just assumed they knew everything and just came in. It's funny. I taught constitutional law to thousands of students over twenty-three years, usually at least 100 per class, and I still remember certain students. Bob Livingston, for example, who almost became Speaker of the House before having to resign.

*You said in the speech that we listened to that if Walker hadn't contracted tuberculosis, that he would have gone to the war and then probably come home to become a psychiatrist. Do you think he would have been comfortable settling into a daily routine with patients?*

Oh yeah, I think so. You know, he used to spend a lot of time at the Waffle House in Covington. He'd go by himself, and he loved it. I do the same thing sometimes, just playing around over here. He'd go in there and just observe, overhear things, maybe talk to strangers, whatnot. I think as a psychiatrist, he would have been unbelievable.

*It seems, from what other people have told me, that he might have been more interested in using the therapy to heal people versus trying to learn what made people tick in order to answer some of his own questions about people and life, the more academic approach.*

I think he would've enjoyed both aspects, but his real interest would have been that person, that one person. As I mentioned in the speech, he had a way of getting to the heart of the matter. That's a lawyer's job. He could do that very well. I didn't really know him well enough when we were growing up to see when he began to outdistance other people. He was always one of the guys, always liked movies, and I remember going up to Chapel Hill to see him. He had a lot of friends, but he was not a standout. I don't think, even at that college level, he struck anybody as being an outstanding scholar or thinker. I think his self-discipline was fantastic.

*LeRoy said that Walker was always disappointed that he didn't serve in World War II, like you mentioned in your speech. LeRoy also said that he wouldn't have enjoyed it, that the military would have driven Walker nuts. What do you think?*

I never thought about it that way, but yeah, I don't think he'd have liked being in the military because of the orders and the structure of the program. But he would have loved being in the war. That required a certain type of discipline that he would have loved. He wouldn't have liked the military any more than I did, but he would have realized that a military-type organization was necessary to fight a war.

I never directly heard him say to anybody how he missed being in World War II, and I'm not sure LeRoy did either. We both just felt it. He used to love to hear my war stories. Sometimes he'd say, "That sounds like a lot of fun," that sort of thing.

*You also mentioned that you always thought Walker was going to be a writer after he had left medicine. I asked LeRoy the same thing because there was such a long gap between medical school and "The*

*Moviegoer" being published. LeRoy said that he was completely surprised by Walker's turning into an author. Do you recall what Walker was up to during that gap between medical school and the first publication?*

Well, Shelby got published before Walker did, and I think that kind of stirred Walker up, the competition of it. It's a good question. I did know during that period that he read all the time at Saranac Lake. I was not surprised that he came up with some deep stuff of his own, but I was so busy with things that I wasn't thinking that much about what he was doing. We were all happy that he was recovering from that damned TB. The next thing I knew, he was married to Bunt.

*Was that a surprise to you?*

Yeah, it sure was. I don't think I'd known Bunt before they were married. I was kind of in and out, you know, during and after the navy.

I may be getting away from the point. I forget whether it was in Covington or here, but I remember when *The Last Gentleman* was published that I said, "Walker, what's the message in this one?" And he said, "Oh, don't ever say that! If people hear that there's a message in it, they'll never buy it!" That tickled me to death.

*So you both spent time rebuilding your lives, then the next thing you know he's married, and then you heard that he had converted to Catholicism. What did you think about that?*

That didn't surprise me. I knew that he'd had a long time lying in that bed at Saranac to think about such things. I don't know which people influenced him toward Catholicism particularly, but he had given religion a great deal of thought. He was, I think, very disturbed by Uncle Will's account of his religious experience in *Lanterns on the Levee*. Uncle Will grew up as a Catholic and then threw it aside. I guess it just didn't fit in with him. Our parents were Presbyterian. My father had been a Sunday school teacher in Birmingham. In Greenville, I don't recall going to Sunday school much or anything really. I just think lying on his bed at Saranac he began thinking it all over and giving it a very thorough review. I can see him thinking, "If I'm going to be religious, I'd better go all the way."

After we moved here, for several years I went on Catholic retreats with him. We'd go to Manresa, a retreat in a little town called Convert, Louisiana, not too far from here. It was beautiful, a lovely place, and we would go over there, Walker and I and maybe a couple of other friends, usually from a Wednesday to a Sunday. We never said a word—there was no talking. There would be sermons and whatnot, but mostly just walking around the gardens and thinking. I used to love it. He never tried to convert me, though —that just wasn't Walker's type. He never made any effort that I was aware of.

*Did you consider it anyway, watching your brother, going to these retreats? Where did you wind up, religiously speaking?*

The few times we've been to church, like when my daughters got married, we've been to the Episcopal church, Trinity Church, out here on Jackson Avenue. I don't remember the last time we went. The minister, or the rector I think they call him, he's a wonderful man named Hill Riddle. Hill asked me once why we didn't come to church more often, and I told him that his sermons were magnificent, but the minute you go into church is like going to a cocktail party without any glasses. It was a social occasion. After church, everybody meets outside and talks and talks and talks. I believe very, very strongly in God, but organized religions thus far have not had much effect on me. I liked the retreats, but that didn't mean that I liked Catholicism. The religious surroundings were nice after the tumult of teaching and business. I used to always end up on Sundays feeling much better than when I started, but organized religions, I've always had some doubts about them. I was influenced greatly by what Uncle Will said in *Lanterns on the Levee*. I used to argue with Walker sometimes. I used to like to dig him about the Catholics. The Catholic priests could not get married, say—I'd ask him why. Episcopal ministers get married, and other people who have very difficult jobs get married. A spouse is supposed to help you. He never gave me a satisfactory answer. He'd start pulling at his nose and say, "Oh, total commitment," and that kind of thing. I just told him I can't buy it. I think he had some doubts about it too. I used to love getting into little arguments with him like that.

I remember that we were at a retreat in Manresa when Jack Kennedy got shot. The theologian in charge called everybody in and announced what had happened. Walker, I think, was stunned more than I was. I was stunned because I knew Jack. I'm not sure I've ever seen Walker hit as hard by any other thing, though. When we left the retreat, Walker had trouble for a while coping with it. He had great respect and admiration for Jack Kennedy. It hit him particularly hard, which kind of surprised me. You hardly ever knew where Walker stood on issues. He never gave out too much. Whether Walker was a liberal or a conservative, I couldn't say. Walker was his own man. If I had to classify him, I'd say a moderate conservative. But then he testified about the Confederate flag flying in a principal's office, and that took a lot of nerve, especially in the climate back then. I used to ask him who he voted for, but I'm not sure liberal or conservative ever fit him. He just called it his way.

*What do you think he got from Catholicism? You mentioned his doubts, as others have, but then he also wound up an oblate with the Abbey. Some folks have said, including a former priest, that Walker was never really a Catholic. Other folks have insisted that he bought the whole thing, hook, line, and sinker.*

Well, he would have loved that those disparate views were held. That would have tickled him, and he would have chuckled over that: "Nobody knows why I am a Catholic." I think he had a very high moral standard, and the Catholic church as he understood it also had a high moral standard, and it didn't have any of the crackpots that you find in the Protestant denominations. If you're serious about religion, this is the one that ought to get your attention. I don't think he had any strong, strong belief in any religious theory over another one. The Christian religion itself was one of the oldest, the best organized, the most literate, with strong foundations, historical, intellectual, and otherwise. I think if one finds a need to be in organized religion, it's the thing to do. If you were to seed religions like you would people in a golf tournament, I think Catholic would be number 1, Episcopal number 2.

I think it surprised him that I would enjoy those Manresa retreats as much as I did, but I think he saw that it was the retreat aspect more than the Catholic aspect that drew me. He never made any attempt to convert me.

*When I spoke with Shelby about this, he said that he never needed a church because he had art to worship. Do you have anything similar?*

That sounds like Shelby. I have an extremely strong view toward morality. For example, all of Clinton's misdoings, to me one far outdistances the others. To me, adultery is the worst sin. If you do have a high moral standard, which I consider I have, you're naturally going to give some thought to religion. Religion's main purpose, as I understand it, is to make you give some thought to a moral life. I remember talking to Walker after one of the retreats about this thing that really gets me, this "born again" theory. I said, "Walker, does that mean that if Sam Giancana comes down from the Mob and says, 'I'm born again,' is that all it takes?" And he'd pull at his nose and say, "Oh, you know, well," and so on. But that's the kind of thing that bothers me about organized religion. If Billy Graham tells me to kneel down and say, "I believe," why do I have to say that to Billy Graham? Why can't I do that on my own? Why do I have to go to church? I can see where, if I needed to have moral standards, I could go to church and see what they are, but I have moral standards, I know them from my own upbringing. I remember Uncle Will sent me to a Presbyterian school. I took Bible every year, the Old Testament and the New Testament and whatnot. I don't think he ever realized how hard they were trying to get me to come forward, which I never would do. I never told him about it because I liked the school a great deal except for that. It was the McCallie School in Chattanooga, Tennessee. But there was heavy pressure on every student there to say, "I believe," and come forward. So I feel I don't need to go to church to live a moral life, and if living a moral life is not good enough to get you where you're supposed to go, then too bad, I missed out. As I say, I don't ever recall going to church when I was in Greenville, and McCallie turned me off to organized religion.

*I see, and I certainly understand. I wonder, now that we've brought up that period of time again, if you'd talk some about the loss of your parents. When I talked with Shelby and LeRoy, they said that your parents' deaths hit you all a bit differently. With you being the youngest, there was some concern that it hit you hardest. Do you have many recollections of your arrival in Greenville, how you coped with the losses? I'm trying to figure out whether these events charted a course for your life. I think that in Walker's novels, the loss of your father and your mother are threads that never leave the stories. I've probably been exposed to too much psychoanalytic theory, but I have to ask if the manner of your mother's death, and your being in the car with her when it went under water, influenced your own course in life, especially your approach to the war and your actions while in the navy.*

I never thought about it that way before. Oh my, well, of course my mother's death struck me the worst because I was in the car with her and I was much older. I was only seven when my father died, and I didn't realize much about what was going on with him. But my mother's death will never leave me. I recall what happened over and over again. I don't—I don't know.

How it affected me, I guess I just don't know. I know it has affected me a great deal. The death of any parent you love is going to affect you. More than her death, I frequently think about her years in Greenville as being unhappy years for her. She was unbelievably grateful to Uncle Will for inviting us all over there, but I don't think she ever quite realized what her place was there. I don't think she was ever that comfortable in Greenville. I don't have any recollections of seeing her smile, have fun, no recollections whatsoever.

I remember her being one of the most beautiful ladies I had ever seen but always wearing a sad expression. It was a very complicated household because I don't think she ever realized whether she was running the house or whether it was Arcile, Louiza the cook—it was like living in a hotel. You never knew who was going to be there for any meal, and people from all over the world would come down there and want to see Uncle Will and learn about the South and whatnot. She just had trouble understanding. I frequently try to think back to Athens, right after my father's death, when we moved to Athens for a year, but I just have almost no recollection of it. I remember enjoying it myself, and I remember being fantastically devoted to my mother's mother, Grandmother Phinizy, where we stayed, but I just have no recollection of my mother, other than being sad. I think she was much loved in Greenville by everyone who knew her, but to have a husband commit suicide, to start off with that. I hope that somewhere along the line we three boys were a source of pleasure to her, and I'm sure we were. I'll never forget once when she was at Uncle Will's house and Walker and LeRoy were arguing and she kind of broke it up crying

—she just couldn't stand it. And I never heard them argue again. I'm sure they have, but I never heard them have harsh words again at all, even back then in their teens. I remember her breaking them apart and being very upset about it. I don't think in the history of the world there have ever been three brothers who got along as well as we did. To have two older brothers I could turn to for any kind of assistance or help, counseling or whatnot, they were always there, Walker and LeRoy both. But I hope we gave some pleasure to her.

*Do you think that the strain on your mother was also a result of earlier problems with depression?*

I have virtually no recollections of my life in Birmingham. I know from reading a book that I was there when my father took his own life, and Walker and LeRoy were off at camp somewhere, but I didn't know what had happened. It was probably years before I realized what caused it and the effects it had on my mother.

*Do you ever go back to Birmingham?*

No, no. I do remember when one of LeRoy's sons got married, he married a girl from Birmingham, and there was a party at the Birmingham Country Club. My father had been the president of that club, he loved to play golf, but that's the only memory I have of being back there, that was quite a while ago. I don't know whether our home is still there or not. Everything has changed so much in this world that I'm sure that I wouldn't recognize anything there. The house was in the country then. It was an absolutely gorgeous home. It had a long, sloping lawn, went right down to the country club road.

*It's not the country anymore. I used to live a few blocks from the house. It's a beautiful area, my favorite part of the whole city. Based on what we've just discussed and what you mentioned that you've read, how did you feel about reading Bertram Wyatt-Brown's book? How did you feel about seeing a book laid out to show the thread of mental illness through so many generations of your family?*

Well, actually, I can't object to it because it's the truth. What my family is blessed with—sure, it's not nice to be reminded of my grandfather killing himself and my father killing himself, but to what extent I've thought about that more because of these books, I don't know. What I have thought about is the greatest thing that happened to my two brothers and myself was my father marrying a Phinizy. I think that brought in some genes that kept us from all being manic depressive. I think that saved Walker, LeRoy, and myself. I don't think that any of us have ever had any suicidal tendencies. I feel I'm very fortunate because my wife also has wonderful genes, so that history of the Percy males, I think, is over. I'm not blaming anybody from way back yonder, but what I'm saying is that pattern is history. I can't hold it against these writers if they want to write about that. It's certainly their prerogative.

*Did it put you off at first?*

Yeah, I had some harsh words earlier with Bertram Wyatt-Brown about some of the things he said about Uncle Will and some other things. Let me read you a letter I wrote to him around 1996:

> Dear Professor Wyatt-Brown:
>
> At the urging of my brother LeRoy, I've read *The House of Percy*. I write to say that I think it's a fine piece of work, and although I inevitably disagree with some of your observations and conclusions, on the whole I find the book to be eminently fair. I've always felt that the toughest job for a writer is a biography, and I now realize that there is a far more formidable task, to wrestle with the saga of a southern family. Congratulations on a superior job.
>
> Sincerely,
> Billups Phinizy Percy

After I sent that letter, I got this back from him:

> Dear Percy,
>
> I'm delighted that you found *The House of Percy* "eminently fair." I've had the impression, ever since the book appeared in 1994, that the members of the Percy family were highly displeased with it. I'd like to reassure you, your brother LeRoy, and anybody else who might think otherwise that I had every intention of treating your family with respect, and even unstinting admiration when that reaction was called for. But since you are the first member of the family to express any opinion about it, positive or negative, directly to me, I am much gratified that one of the prominent Percys has reached such a generous and, for me, most welcome conclusion. Indeed, I wish some of the reviewers who criticized me for being

either inappropriately candid or too reticent and unforthcoming had agreed with you. All reviews were positive, I might add, except for the *New York Times*. Thank you very much for your comments, and I assure you that they are most appreciated.

Sincerely,

Bertram Wyatt-Brown

*He seems like a good man. I heard him speak, and I spoke with him briefly about his work.*

I'll never understand how he did all that research. It was an enormous project.

*What specifically in the book did you have objections about? Was it all over Uncle Will or what?*

I think it was in part about Uncle Will, probably. It is a very candid book. But I believe in the First Amendment. As I say, though, I'm particularly impressed by the research. How anyone would get that interested in another family, I just can't understand it.

*I think he saw what a number of people have seen, that your family has one hell of a story. I'm sure he just started looking and found out that there was a story like this all the way back. What are the ages of your children?*

They're all in their forties. The youngest is 40, then 43, 44, and 45. Two sons, two daughters. We have grandchildren now. One daughter lives in Covington, and she brings over her two children every week. My other daughter lives in Atlanta, and they have two children. Each daughter has a boy and a girl, so we have four grandchildren. I've always worried about the Percy males because Walker didn't have any sons. My two sons have not married yet, but Le-Roy's had sons and grandsons now.

*Speaking of carrying on the name, I wonder if I could switch gears and ask you how Walker broke the news to you that he was fatally ill.*

I don't—I just don't—the thing I remember is that when I did find out he had serious problems, sometimes he'd drive in and I would meet him on the River Road. We'd meet and chat, and then he'd go to the hospital. I do remember—there was one incident—there was one incident when he was having difficulty. I found out who the doctor was that he was seeing in Covington, so I drove over there and went to see the doctor and chatted with him about Walker's situation. He indicated that it wasn't as bad as it could have been, and after that, I came out, and who comes in but Walker and Bunt. And Walker said, "What the hell are you doing over here?" And I said, "Well, Walker, I keep asking you about your condition and you never tell me anything, so I thought I'd come see the doctor." And Walker said, "Well, what did he say?" and I said, "That you seem to be doing better," and he said it was okay, and I left. But when I first heard about it, I don't know. At the end, LeRoy and Sarah came down and stayed with Bunt, and my wife and I went over every day.

*There has been some very good work done on the life of your brother, and a lot has been said about what sort of man he was. Is there a final comment you'd like to share about him?*

Well, he was obviously a very distinguished writer of fiction and non-fiction, but he will be remembered by all those who knew him not as a great writer but as a wonderful person. The fact that he was a writer—so what? It was because of what he was, not what he did, that we loved him. Among his countless attributes, he was one of the most honest men you'll meet. I can't imagine Walker lying about anything. I don't think he ever did—it wasn't in him to tell it other than how it was. Honesty was a pretty important characteristic about him, among many. I just wonder if anybody has ever been as fortunate to have an oldest brother like I had. I hope other people have, but I'm not sure that anybody ever has. I'll close on that.

Now for some reason, the Orleans Club asked me to speak about my brother back in 1991, and I thought you might like to hear what I said about Walker then. At that point, my memory was pretty good. I'm fortunate I have a memory at all now! [Phin plays a recording of the speech, a transcription of which follows.]

The only problem I had in preparing for you all was trying to capture the highlights of a relationship that spanned almost seventy years. It's difficult to do in a fairly short time frame. What I want to convey to you is what sort of a person he was. I apologize to you because I haven't rehearsed. The way I operate is that I sort of ad lib and proceed in an order, in this case chronologically. I would like to start by reading a letter I wrote to the paper after Walker died to give you an idea at the outset of how I felt about Walker.

I have read just about all the published works of my brother, Walker Percy, and I am aware of only one misstatement of fact in his writing. In his magnificent introduction to the paperback edition of William Alexander Percy's *Lanterns on the Levee*, Walker closes by stating, "I owe him a debt which cannot be paid." What I think Walker had in mind here was that for a bachelor to take on the chore of raising three young sons of his favorite cousin after the tragic death of their father and mother, Uncle Will, as we called him, not only set an awesome example of self-sacrifice and family loyalty but also tried to instill in each of us a sense of morality and compassion and an idea of what was truly worthwhile in this life. We three brothers do owe this great man a debt of immense proportions, but I know that Uncle Will would agree that Walker has paid his debt. He has done it not merely by the sustained excellence of his writing but more importantly by the life he lived. Unselfishness, humility, sensitivity, helping others, including countless aspiring young writers whom Walker continued to counsel even after his own physical pain became so intense that he could no longer continue his own writing—these were the hallmarks of Walker Percy's life. Walker, the debt has been paid in full.

You can gather that the first ten years of my life were quite turbulent. My father died when I was seven, my mother died when I was ten, and so I have really no recollection of my relationship then with my two brothers. Walker was six years older than I was, LeRoy was five years older. Aside from the tragic circumstances that pervaded our lives was the fact that during the teen years and the preteens, five or six years was like a generation. They hung out with their crowd, I hung out with my crowd, and I didn't see much of them except at meals. In fact, the first time I remember an encounter with Walker was after my mother died, when we were orphaned and my Uncle Will legally adopted us. He arranged a succession of elderly aunts to come in and run the household. I was about eleven, and Walker seventeen. I came home from school one afternoon and put my books away and got ready to get with my crowd. We'd go out and play marbles—marbles were very big then in Greenville—or baseball, whatever. I was just leaving and Walker comes in and he says, "Phin, have you got a few minutes?" and I said, "Yeah, yeah." So he said, "Let's take a walk around the block." I thought uh-oh, I don't know about this. Walker had a habit that he continued all his life that when he was nervous, he would pull at his nose, repeatedly and quickly. He was pulling his nose then. So we started out walking, and he said, "Look, Phin, you know about the birds and the bees, don't you? You know, the facts of life." And I said, "Walker, I think so." He said, "You know how babies are made, don't you?" I said, "I believe so." And he just said, "Good, then we can go on back," and he turned around and headed back to the house, just a-pulling his nose. What had happened was that Walker had been assigned to the task of giving me the facts of life, and so I suppose it was the shortest course ever given in sex education.

Moving on a few years to 1939. During that period from 1933 to 1939, I saw very little of Walker. I went to prep school, he went to the University of North Carolina, I went to summer camp, and so on. The next thing I recall is when I entered the United States Naval Academy in 1942. Uncle Will made some decisions which puzzled some of us at the time. Walker never understood why he was sent to medical school, and I certainly never understood why I was sent to the Naval Academy. So I got there about the end of June in '39. I don't know if any of you have ever seen it—I've never been back since graduation—but it looked like a prison. There were walls around it, making it hard to get out, and I didn't know anybody, and we were sometimes treated like it was a prison.

Well, when I got there, there was nobody but the plebes and some chief petty officers. The upperclassmen were all on summer cruises on battleships and destroyers. So the summer went on, and it wasn't unbearable, it was just dull. I remember most of all marching with a rifle, and I couldn't understand what a naval officer was doing marching with a rifle. I can also remember rowing boats up and down the river in Annapolis. But finally the summer was over, then leave was over for the upperclassmen who'd been on their cruises. They got a month's vacation after their cruise was over and then came back in October, and that's when the show really started. We had dreaded it the whole summer. Of course, they were irritable, their vacation was over and they were back at the school, and who do they take it out on but the plebes. I can remember well the first night they were back, at the meal. The tables in the mess hall were rectangular and held maybe twenty people, most of whom were upperclassmen. The plebes sat maybe three or four to a table, in the middle. An upperclassman said, "Okay, sound off," and we were supposed to call out our names. It came to me and I said, "Midshipman Billups Phinizy Percy, 4th Class." This guy almost fell out of his chair in convulsions, along with some of the other upperclassmen. He said, "What the hell kind of a name is that?" And I said, "Well, I didn't have anything to do with it." And he said, "That may be your name, but you are Al, get it? A-L, for the rest of the year." And that's sort of dehumanizing, to take your name away from you. But that was only the beginning.

I didn't like anything about the Naval Academy. I didn't like the hazing, and it was pretty fierce. All the paddling and doing push-ups. We were the class of '43, so we were always required to do 43 push-ups while singing "Anchors Aweigh." But most of all, the things you dreaded were the meals. There'd always be some upperclassman taking his bad mood out on you. They'd tell you to "shove off," which meant you had to take your chair and put it under the table and eat your meal kneeling. And he'd say, "While you're at it, eat a square meal," which meant you had to move your fork in a square pattern from the plate to your mouth and back for every bite. Well, I got fed up with it, and on top of it all—understand that things have changed—the academic program was miserable. There was a rule that in every class, every day, you had to get a grade. And these teachers were all former naval cadets who had come back to teach, and every day they'd say, "Gentlemen, do you have any questions?" Well, there was no point in asking these people any questions, you weren't going to get any clarification. You could try to stall, but you knew you were going to get a test before it was over that day. So after about five minutes of questions and some strange answers, you took a test, and that was class. I was amazed later on when I went to Sewanee and then finally got to the University of Virginia Law School, and the professors were actually explaining things.

I had wanted to go to the University of North Carolina like my brothers and be an SAE. I had been to Walker's graduation, and I loved the place. But Uncle Will, he saw early on that we were going to get into a war. He tried to enlist himself, at fifty-one years of age. He thought the Naval Academy would be the right place for me. Well, I called Walker in mid-October. He was in Columbia Medical School in New York, and I told him, "Walker, I want you to listen. I have written a very good letter of resignation, and I'd like your comments on it." And it was about a page long, and I wish I had saved it because it was a nice piece of work. And so I read it, and Walker waited until I finished, and then he said, "Gee, I don't blame you. I wouldn't put up with that, no way in the world. But why don't you do this. Why don't you wait until November and see if it gets any worse." So November came around, and I called Walker again, and he said, "I tell you the truth, I don't see how you stayed there this long. Why don't you do this. You get leave in December. Let's talk about it at Christmas." So I went home for Christmas, and I don't believe I'd ever had a better time in my life. There were a lot of parties, and the young ladies seemed to really like the Annapolis uniform, and I really had quite a time. Well, anyway, Walker and I never got around to talking about it, and then came January and I was back at it, and I called him again. He said, "Well, I guess you'd better get on out. But look at it this way. The upperclassmen are just like they were. They're taking it all out on you, and you feel bad because you just came back from a great Christmas. Call me in February. And you also told me you had a chance of getting on the tennis team in March. Why don't you just wait until March and see if you get on the tennis team, and then you can sit at a special table for the athletes and get away from all that." Well, I made the tennis team, I didn't resign, plebe year was soon over, and I went on and graduated. And the greatest thing that happened was that because of the coming war, we graduated in three years instead of four, going to school on Saturdays and summers. But I can tell you that there is not any question that, had it not been for Walker, I would've resigned.

Now he could've said, "Look, don't bother me with your problems. I have problems of my own." But he wasn't like that, even though he disliked medical school even more than I disliked Annapolis. Walker was the greatest listener I have ever known. Usually while we listen we're thinking about what we're going to do or say, but he listened. And then he'd get right to the heart of the matter. He nursed me through nine months of the Naval Academy, and it was like leading somebody through a minefield. And I'll never forget it. If I had resigned, I would have probably ended up a buck private, shoveling manure in Louisiana somewhere, and I would've had to explain for the rest of my life to my family and my son why I was a quitter. If it hadn't been for Walker, I would've been in that situation. Instead, I had what I think was a very successful career as a naval officer.

Now let's move on to Christmas 1941. This is right after Pearl Harbor, and I was due to graduate in June of '42. Walker had graduated med school and was interning at Bellevue, and we went home for the holidays. Of course, as I think many of you have realized now, war is a very exciting thing. There's a lot of bad things about war, but it's exciting. The excitement was in the air then, about two weeks after Pearl Harbor. And the house was full of people. The thing that I noticed was that my Uncle Will was always in his pajamas and his bathrobes. What I didn't know, but LeRoy and Walker knew, was that he'd had a cerebral hemorrhage shortly before Christmas, and he knew he was dying. There was no way to detect that. He was charming, gracious, lively, funny. The only thing I noticed was that sometimes he'd forget names. He'd even forget my name, but then he'd laugh it off and say his memory was at half-attention. Then I got back to the Academy after Christmas, and three weeks later I got a phone call, and I heard, "This is Walker. Uncle Will has died." Then a few minutes later, "Are you there?" I'd never had anything hit me like that. When my mother and father died, I was too young to really appreciate the enormity of the situation. But the man I knew who had loved and protected me for ten years, at fifty-six years of age, was gone. Walker said, "The funeral is tomorrow. I'll fly down from New York, and you get a taxi to Washington, and we'll fly back together." I mention this because if I hadn't been with Walker on that flight down, I don't know what I'd have done. It was nothing he said particularly, it was just being with him that made the tragedy bearable. We talked about Uncle Will and the things he had done, how he'd taken on three young boys when he could've done so many other things he wanted to do, traveling and such. So Walker got me through that time.

So the funeral was over, I went back to Annapolis, he went back to New York, and right before I graduated in June, I got word that Walker had come down with tuberculosis while he was interning. I was assigned to PT boats, so I picked up a squadron in Connecticut and we took the boat to New York, and Walker was still in Bellevue, but this time as a patient. I went to see him and he looked bad, coughing a lot, and we chatted about the war and whatnot. And his room at Bellevue looked out over the East River, and I told him that tomorrow the PT boats would be doing a speed run down the river and he could watch it. I didn't see him again, but I learned that he did watch it and got a kick out of it.

Then three years passed while I was engaged in fighting the Japanese. LeRoy was in a B-26 bomber, based in France, and he fought the Germans for three years. Walker spent three years fighting tuberculosis in a sanitorium in upstate New York. I believe it's fair to state that the biggest disappointment in Walker's life was that he couldn't participate in World War II. He felt as strongly about the Nazi menace as Uncle Will had. On top of that, he was flat on his back, not knowing if he was going to live or not.

The bright side of it, if there is a bright side, is this: If he hadn't gotten TB, he would've gotten into the service and I'm sure served very honorably, and I think the chances are 100 to 1 that after the war he'd have gone back to medicine, become a doctor, a psychiatrist perhaps, and he would've been one of the world's greatest psychoanalysts. Instead of that, for three years he lay flat on his back, and all he did was read and think. And that was when the seeds of becoming a writer began to grow. And after he recovered from TB, I don't think there was any doubt in his mind that he was going to become a writer. And so without the TB, we can at least say, I'm quite sure the world would have been deprived of the writing of Walker Percy. He would've probably written a few arcane articles that nobody could have understood, but he would not have been a novelist, for sure.

I had already gone from PT boats to submarines, and then after the war was over, I went back to the United States and then to Panama, where I stayed until 1947, when I resigned from the navy. To me it was like practicing after the game was over. I didn't want to be an admiral anyway, so I got out of the navy and went to the

U.S. It so happened that Walker had recovered more or less from TB and had gotten married to Bunt in 1946 in New Orleans. He and Bunt were going to spend the summer of 1947 at Uncle Will's summer house near Sewanee, a beautiful place near a valley. So I went up to spend the summer with them. I remember that Walker and Bunt and I had lots of visitors, including Allen Tate and Caroline Gordon, who were great friends of Walker's and fine writers.

I had a wonderful summer. I went to summer school to supplement my so-called education at the Naval Academy. The point I want to make about that summer is this: Somewhere along the line, Walker—Walker would always kind of slip up on you, and he said, "Do you want to take a look at this?" And he handed me a thick manuscript that said, "*The Charterhouse* by Walker Percy." Well, I read about thirty pages, and I went to Walker and I said, "Now Walker, look. I'm not a literary critic. You write beautifully, there's no question about it, but it doesn't get me. You don't get anywhere. It's not moving, and I can't go on." As I recall, he was describing a group of people at a party in great detail. He was describing what they were wearing—creases in the men's pants and the lace and such. This went on and on. And I said this to him, and it was 1,100 pages, and he said, "You're probably right." The book was rejected, and I mean rejected out of hand. And I found out later that he wrote another novel, *The Gramercy Winner* I believe it was, and that was rejected out of hand. I tell you this because at the end, I want to tell you why I think, after these rebuffs, Walker persisted in becoming a novelist.

Walker and Bunt left Sewanee and went to New York. I liked it so much that I moved in with some friends and stayed, not to get a degree but to take some courses I didn't have at Annapolis. So in '48, some friends of mine and I went to Europe, North Africa, and came back. And somewhere along the line I saw Walker, I don't remember if it was in Greenville or New Orleans or where, but I do remember this: He said, "What are you going to do with the rest of your life?" And I told him I'd made up my mind to apply to Columbia graduate school and get a degree in English and I'm going to be a writer. And he said, "I have two comments: Number 1, if you're going to be a writer, don't go to school to be a writer. Get a pencil and a piece of paper and start writing. Secondly, if there's anything in this world you can do, do it rather than be a writer. It's the loneliest, most depressing work in the world."

Of course, in 1948, Walker had a right to be depressed. He'd had two novels and had not gotten either one of them published. And I took his advice and entered Virginia Law School. A lot of people who don't know what they want to do go to law school. So I did that and got out, graduated in '52. Sometimes I wonder if I had asked Walker that same question fifteen years later, after he had won the National Book Award, whether he'd have given me the same answer. I think he would have. Depression for an established writer is a different type of depression. It's not the depression of having your books rejected; it's the depression of having an unfavorable book review because you leave yourself open to the critics. I will never forget, after I think *Lancelot* was reviewed in the *New York Times* with a savage review, not only on the book but on Walker, calling him a chauvinist and such, and I have never seen Walker so mad. So it may be that he would've given me the same answer even then.

I got married in '53, and in 1954 my wife and I moved into an apartment in New Orleans and we've been here ever since. One of the great things about living in New Orleans is that we saw Walker and Bunt regularly and we would go and see them on weekends, or Walker and Bunt would come over for dinner and a movie, for Walker was a moviegoer himself. In addition, a group of us started having lunch together, which we continued right up until Walker's death. So I saw Walker a great deal for the next thirty-five years.

Walker and I used to kid each other a bit about writers. He tried to get me to read a book called *The Sound and the Fury*, and I had to tell him I just couldn't make it. With sentences three or four pages long, no punctuation, not knowing who's talking to whom, I told him I just couldn't keep going. And he said, "Well okay, but I'll say this for your man"—and by "your man," he meant Ernest Hemingway—and he said, "Ernest Hemingway can probably describe a young lady getting out of a taxicab in Paris better than any writer who ever lived." And I told him to back off, and the truth was that Walker did acknowledge that Hemingway had talent, particularly as a master of the short story. But the one thing we both agreed on was that the most underrated novelist of the century was Raymond Chandler. The trouble with Raymond Chandler was that he became known as a mystery writer, with his chief character being a private eye, Philip Marlowe.

There's been a lot written about Walker. In all of them I find listed as the major influences on Walker as being Kierkegaard, Heidegger, Proust, and Sartre, all of whom are existentialists. Well, I have never read anything by any of those four people. I don't know what an existentialist is—I should, but I don't. I wouldn't know one if I saw him at high noon on the courthouse steps. But Walker, I understand, was an existentialist. Maybe it means that he had a fierce regard for man's fate. But anyway, it's my position that the person who influenced Walker more than anyone else to become a novelist, to persevere for fifteen years after two rejections, was Albert Camus, the Algerian writer who was born about the same time as Walker. It was Camus who convinced Walker that the novel could be a vehicle for a philosophical discussion. In other words, the novel is a prose narrative with a plot and with characters who interact, but with Camus and with Walker it was more. There was a second level of communication in Camus's novels— *The Plague*, *The Stranger*, *The Fall*—I read these and discussed them with Walker. The casual reader might just get the story, but the careful reader would come out with something more. That was certainly true of Walker's novels. Alienation of man, despair, his search for what life was all about, the strange circumstance that man knows everything about science, technology, and the universe but knows nothing about himself, these things were part and parcel of Walker's prose. And I close by stating that Linda Hobson has written a book called *Understanding Walker Percy*. I don't think anyone will ever write a book called *Understanding Stephen King* or *Understanding Danielle Steele*. They tell good stories, but you get what you see and that's it. Not with Walker.

# Bibliography

Allen, William Rodney. *Walker Percy: A Southern Wayfarer*. Jackson: University
Press of Mississippi, 1986.

Backscheider, Paula R. *Reflections on Biography*. Oxford: Oxford University
Press, 1999.

Baker, Lewis. *The Percys of Mississippi: Politics and Literature in the New
South*. Baton Rouge: Louisiana State University Press, 1983.

Baron, Samuel H. *Introspection in Biography: The Biographer's Quest for Self-
Awareness*. Hillsdale, N.Y.: Analytic, 1985.

Barringer, Nikki. Personal interview. 29 September 1999.

Barrios, Lee. Personal interview. 30 September 1999.

Boulware, James. Personal interview. 27 September 1999.

Campbell, Will. Personal interview. 11 June 2000.

Caro, Robert A. *Extraordinary Lives: The Art and Craft of American Biography*.
New York: American Heritage, 1986.

Coles, Robert. *Walker Percy: An American Search*. Boston: Little, Brown, 1978.

Cyprian, Carrie. Personal interview. 29 September 1999.

D'Arc, Sister Jeanne. Personal interview. 30 September 1999.

Dupuy, Edward J. *Autobiography in Walker Percy: Repetition, Recovery, and
Redemption*. Baton Rouge: Louisiana State University Press, 1996.

Edel, Leon. *Telling Lives: The Biographer's Art*. Philadelphia: University of
Pennsylvania Press, 1981.

Epstein, William H. *Contesting the Subject: Essays in the Postmodern Theory
and Practice of Biography and Biographical Criticism*. West Lafayette, Ind.:
Purdue University Press, 1991.

Faulkner, Jim. *Talking about William Faulkner*. Baton Rouge: Louisiana State
University Press, 1996.

Faust, Rhoda. Personal interview. 1 October 1999.

Foote, Shelby. Personal interview. 9 June 2000.

France, Peter. *Mapping Lives: The Uses of Biography*. Oxford: Oxford
University Press, 2002.

Frick, Leroy. Personal interview. 2 October 1999.

Hobson, Linda. *Understanding Walker Percy*. Columbia: University of South
Carolina Press, 1988.

————. *Walker Percy: A Comprehensive Descriptive Bibliography*. New Orleans: Faust, 1988.

Holroyd, Michael. *Works on Paper: The Craft of Biography and Autobiography*. London: Little, Brown, 2002.

Honan, Park. *Authors' Lives: On Literary Biography and the Arts of Language*. New York: St. Martin's, 1990.

Jolly, Margaretta, ed. *Encyclopedia of Life Writing: Autobiographical and Biographical Forms*. London: Fitzroy Dearborn, 2001.

Kendall, Paul Murray. *The Art of Biography*. New York: Norton, 1985.

LaCour, Judy. Personal interview. 30 September 1999.

Lawson, Lewis A. *Following Percy: Essays on Walker Percy's Work*. Troy, N.Y.: Whitson, 1987.

————. *Still Following Percy*. Jackson: University of Mississippi Press, 1995.

Lawson, Lewis A., and Victor Kramer, eds. *Conversations with Walker Percy*. Jackson: University of Mississippi Press, 1985.

————. *More Conversations with Walker Percy*. Jackson: University of Mississippi Press, 1993.

Meyers, Jeffrey. *The Craft of Literary Biography*. London: MacMillan, 1985.

Nadel, Ira B. *Biography: Fiction, Fact, and Form*. London: MacMillan, 1984.

Percy, LeRoy. Personal interview. 9 June 2000.

Percy, Phin. Personal interview. 18 December 2000.

Percy, Walker. *Lancelot*. New York: Farrar, Straus, 1977.

————. *The Last Gentleman*. New York: Farrar, Straus, 1966.

————. *Lost in the Cosmos: The Last Self-Help Book*. New York: Farrar, Straus, 1983.

————. *Love in the Ruins: The Adventures of a Bad Catholic at a Time Near the End of the World*. New York: Farrar, Straus, 1971.

————. *The Message in the Bottle: How Queer Man Is, How Queer Language Is, and What One Has to Do with the Other*. New York: Farrar, Straus, 1975.

————. *The Moviegoer*. New York: Knopf, 1961.

————. *The Second Coming*. New York: Farrar, Straus, 1980.

————. *Signposts in a Strange Land*. Edited by Patrick Samway. New York: Farrar, Straus, 1991.

————. *The Thanatos Syndrome*. New York: Farrar, Straus, 1987.

Percy, Walker, and Kenneth L. Ketner. *A Thief of Peirce: The Letters of Kenneth Laine Ketner and Walker Percy*. Edited by Patrick Samway. Jackson: University of Mississippi Press, 1995.

Percy, William Alexander. *Lanterns on the Levee*. Baton Rouge: Louisiana State University Press, 1974.

Quinlan, Kieran. *Walker Percy: The Last Catholic Novelist*. Baton Rouge: Louisiana State University Press, 1996.

Samway, Patrick. *Walker Percy: A Life*. New York: Farrar, Straus, 1997.

Smith, John "Red," Jr. Personal interview. 29 September 1999.

Tolson, Jay. *Pilgrim in the Ruins: A Life of Walker Percy*. New York: Simon and Schuster, 1992.

———, ed. *The Correspondence of Shelby Foote and Walker Percy*. New York: Center for Documentary Studies, 1997.

Wyatt-Brown, Bertram. *The House of Percy: Honor, Melancholy, and Imagination in a Southern Family*. New York: Oxford University Press, 1994.

———. *The Literary Percys: Family History, Gender, and the Southern Imagination*. Athens: University of Georgia Press, 1994.

# Index

Vonnegut, Kurt, Jr., 35

*Walker Percy: A Life* (Samway), 1–4, 95
Welty, Eudora, 41, 143
"Why I Live Where I Live" (Percy), 8

World War II: and LeRoy Percy, 102–7, 125, 129; and Phin Percy, 102–7, 155–58, 161
Wyatt-Brown, Bertram: *House of Percy, The*, 2, 3, 167–68